A LONG JOURNEY HOME

STEVIERAY HANSEN

with
MELANIE HEMRY

ALMOND TREE
PUBLISHING

Edited by Robin Patchen at Robin's Red Pen

Formatted by Christopher P.N. Maselli at WritingMomentum.com

Cover by Ryan Kirkpatrick Design

ISBN# 978-0-692-04746-0

Copyright © 2018 by StevieRay Hansen

Almond Tree Publishing
Edmond, Oklahoma

Some names have been changed.

PRAISE FOR A LONG JOURNEY HOME

If you're facing the impossible and want to be reminded that God can do anything—read this book! It will take you on a white-knuckle ride that proves God can take your biggest messes and turn them into masterpieces of His grace. StevieRay Hansen's story will not only keep you turning the pages, it will inspire you to believe that no matter how badly you've been hurt, no matter how far from God's perfect will for your life you may have wandered, He loves you...and He can help you find your way home.

— GINA LYNNES, NEW YORK TIMES BEST-SELLING
GHOSTWRITER

I'm honored to be numbered among StevieRay's friends. I'll never forget sitting outside his home overlooking the sweeping vista of his ranch as he told me his incredible journey searching for what most of us take for granted. Home. Love. Support. I sat on the edge of my chair while he talked. I cried. I laughed. When he finished I said, "You've got to write a book!" I'm thrilled that he put his story in print. It will warm your heart and give you hope for yourself and everyone who needs forgiveness and second chances.

— CHRISTOPHER GRAY, PRESIDENT/CEO TRIPLE J
CONSULTING

StevieRay Hansen's story is a compelling page-turner and a testament to God's amazing grace and ability to use all broken vessels for His glory.

— RENE GUTTERIDGE, AUTHOR, SCREENWRITER AND HEAD WRITER AT SKIT GUYS STUDIOS

The story of StevieRay's life is inspiring and riveting. If you've ever thought about giving up, this renaissance cowboy will challenge you to dust yourself off and keep on keepin' on.

— CHRISTOPHER P.N. MASELLI, BEST-SELLING AUTHOR

CONTENTS

To my wife, Laura, who has gently and lovingly gone to great lengths to understand a dyslexic, under-educated child of God. And especially for being the most important part of what it means to be home.

1

MARRIED TO THE MOB

The sun smiled down from a stunning blue sky like a benediction as I entered the rodeo arena in Redlands, California that day. A rodeo clown with a big red nose and oversized cowboy hat slapped me on the back as he passed. I tipped my hat to him, grateful for the clowns who risked their lives for us. After dropping my war bag, I climbed onto the fence and watched as my partner Buck Tally prepared to mount the bull he'd drawn. I drank in the sights and sounds. I loved the smell of horses, hay, and fresh turned dirt. The announcer's voice echoed through the arena as he introduced Buck.

The bull torpedoed out of the chute, kicking and twisting on sharp hooves. He tossed his head, and I wished I could capture the moment forever. Illuminated against the afternoon sun, I saw his silhouette freeze-framed in a single still shot of motion. He was a magnificent animal, and Buck was one of the best cowboys I knew.

Still, Buck never stood a chance. That bull tossed him like yesterday's leftovers. The crowd roared their approval at Buck's courage as he picked himself up and scrambled toward the fence while the rodeo clown attracted the bull's attention. I watched my friend until he reached safety. Buck and the guys we traveled with were like family. We rode in the Rodeo Cowboys Association, which later became the Professional Rodeo Cowboys Association. We worked a lot of jackpot rodeos, where fifty guys got together and split the pot. Very few professional cowboys showed up to those, so we always cleaned up. Afterwards, we'd hit our next professional rodeo. We rode in Cheyenne, Houston, Fort Worth, Oklahoma City, Las Vegas, and all over California. We even rode in Madison Square Garden. With all those rodeos in all those cities, we cobbled together a good living.

But just like riding broncs, finances went up and down. When things were good, we stayed in hotels. When they weren't so good, we slept in our truck. We'd come to Redlands from Phoenix hoping to make big bucks. Unfortunately, we weren't making enough at this rodeo to pay for our gas.

I slipped outside the arena and found a pay phone—a sure sign I'd been doing the one thing I tried to avoid. *Thinking.* Being back in California allowed memories of my family to break through my defenses like a cat burglar. My heart galloped and my palms felt moist as I inserted quarters to dial the number, always hopeful that things had changed. I stared at my reflection in the smudged glass of the phone booth. I was twenty-five years old. I needed to get a grip.

My mother answered. Her voice hard as ever.

"Mama? It's me."

"I know who you are. What do you want?"

"Well...I...um. I just wanted to apologize...you know...for everything. I'm sorry."

"You sure are."

I stared at the phone and listened to the dial tone.

It was the luck of the draw that determined if we rode a bareback bronc or a saddle bronc in each event. I'd drawn a saddle bronc and was the last of my group to ride. "You've got to cover your horse!" Buck said. "We've all been bucked off, and we need the money!"

I'd put my chaps on and was back behind the chute when I looked up to see a beautiful woman staring at me. We locked eyes, and she didn't blink. She was tall, lean, and carried herself with regal poise. Her brunette hair had been kissed with streaks of blonde. She watched me with luminous brown eyes. Bold as brass.

Nobody could compartmentalize the way I could. I had an uncanny ability to shut out everything around me and hyper-focus on one single thing. But there wasn't a man alive who could shut out those eyes, that face, and that body. I felt her gaze follow me like a caress. My knees felt weak and my pulse hammered in my throat as I climbed into the chute.

My head wasn't in the game, and the horse knew it. He bolted from the chute like his tail was on fire and bucked like he was possessed. I'd left my head, with its tongue hanging out, over by the fence watching that woman. My body tried to ride on automatic pilot, but it seemed as though I'd just gotten my boots into the stirrups when he bucked me off. I landed with my face in the dirt. Scrambling to my feet, I flew toward her as though drawn by some irresistible, unseen force.

Her eyes never left me as I made my way.

"What are you doing?" I asked.

"Hoping to have coffee with you."

Like I said: bold as brass.

Buck and the guys had loaded the truck and were ready to leave. I walked over to them. "I need an hour." I headed back to her, listening to their whistles and cat calls as I walked away. I took off my chaps and put them into my war bag before holding out my hand to her.

"Name's StevieRay."

3

She put a hand as soft as warm butter into mine and held it for a beat.

"Luann," she said. "Come on, I'll drive."

I followed her to a yellow 450 SEL Mercedes. I took one look at it, brushed dirt off my clothes, and settled into the soft leather seat. I looked at her, looked at her car, and knew I was out of my league. I figured I might as well come clean.

"Look, I'm a broke cowboy. Between me and my buddies, we probably have a hundred bucks."

She turned those eyes on me again and smiled. "Not a problem." Reaching into her purse, she pulled out a wad of cash and shoved it into my hand.

They were all hundreds.

"Where'd you get this kind of money?"

"I just retired from a modeling career in New York City." Her smiled blinded me. "It was very lucrative." Like most models, she'd started young. I figured her for about twenty-four or twenty-five now. Over the hill in modeling years.

We got a booth at Denny's and ordered coffee. I'd never met anyone like her and felt alive in every molecule of my body. It reminded me of how I felt riding bulls or broncos. I felt like I did riding in a rodeo, but more so. As if someone had plugged that feeling into ten million volts of live electricity.

Like that.

I tarried for as long as I could before leaving town with my buddies. We were headed for a rodeo in Texas, but we hadn't gotten far before I announced, "I'm hungry. Let's stop and eat."

"You're not hungry," Buck said without so much as slowing the truck.

"I'm hungry!"

All the guys chimed in. "You just want to stop and call that woman!"

The anger always simmering below my calm exterior threatened to erupt. Before it could, I caught Buck's eye. He was laughing. Fine. I knew there was no point in trying to fool them. They knew me too well. I stewed for a while before blurting out the truth.

"Come on! Did you *see* her?"

They all burst out laughing. They had, in fact, gotten a good look. They pulled over at the next rest stop so I could call her. I'd only just met the woman, but for the first time in my life, I believed I was going to experience love.

Over the next few months, we rode in rodeos in Texas, Illinois, and Kentucky. During that time, Luann and I spent hours on the phone. Several times she flew across country to see me. One night I put my boot down with my buddies. "Pick a rodeo in California!" They did, and the next day we headed for Orange, California.

A sky the color of sapphire was the perfect backdrop. Luann looked like a mirage, shimmering in the afternoon sun. No matter how many times I'd seen her, her beauty took my breath away. We were both tall, and when I folded her into my arms, it felt as though God had designed her as a perfect fit.

I'd gotten used to eyes the color of Belgium chocolate following my every move. It wasn't just that I knew she was watching as I climbed into the chute to mount. I felt her gaze like an electrical current. I hadn't experienced much happiness until I started riding in rodeos. I paused for a moment, removing the blinders from my mind and letting it roam through the memories of my life, looking for happiness.

None except for the few years as a child when we'd lived in Little Dixie, Kentucky. I'd had friends there, and together we'd climbed fences and ridden cows. I'd learned to ride horses, to hunt and to fish. And I had some happy memories with my grandparents. That was it for happiness until I entered my first rodeo.

Now, seated on my mount, the smell of horses and rich, dark earth made me happy. My buddies watching from the sidelines gave me a kind of comfort I hadn't known since Little Dixie. Knowing Luann was with them sent thrills of joy coursing through my veins. I'd never used drugs, so I didn't have a frame of reference, but I already suspected that Luann was more addictive than heroin.

The announcer called my name, the chute opened, and I felt one with the horse, with Luann, and with the world. The ride felt orchestrated. Inspired. It was as though I knew what the horse was thinking. I prepared for every twist, kick, and buck. For those eight seconds, nothing existed except joy. Every memory, every hurt, and every rejection I'd ever experienced faded into oblivion.

That was why I rode. Not for the purse. Not for the applause. I rode for those moments of total abandon. I would have done it for free if that's what it took. But every time Luann left, it felt as though a part of me left with her. I felt pulled between the two loves of my life. I couldn't imagine giving either of them up.

On Thanksgiving, I pulled up a chair to a feast prepared by Buck's mother. I rotated among my buddies, spending time with them and their families. No matter which friends' family I was with, the conversation with his mother never varied. "StevieRay, are you still estranged from your parents?"

"Yes, Ma'am."

"I told you to call and apologize."

"Yes, ma'am. I did."

Buck's mother went a step further. "Well, you've got to accept that you're a terrible person. This relationship problem? It's all on you. You go see them and make sure you say it that way."

"Yes, ma'am." I gave up telling them that I'd called and apologized upwards of fifty times.

I'd never missed a year riding in the rodeo at Pomona, California, which was only forty miles from where my parents lived. I hadn't seen them in years but decided that if I could ride bulls and broncos, I could work up the courage to visit my parents.

When Dad answered the phone, I jumped right in. "I'm in the area and thought I'd stop by for a visit."

"Well...I guess we could meet you at McDonald's."

They wouldn't let me in their house.

My brother Wayne didn't show up. Mom, Dad, and I sat in the small metal booth in McDonald's. They'd aged, but nothing else seemed to have changed.

"You're good for nothing, StevieRay." My father set down his Big Mac. "I've said it before and I'll say it again. You'll end up in prison. Mark my words."

"Do you have any idea how embarrassed we are of you?" Mom asked, her eyes as cold and hard as icicles. I'd had enough.

"No, ma'am." I stood. "It was good seeing y'all. I've got to hit the road, but before I do, I'd just like to say I'm sorry. You know, for everything." I refused to hang my head like a whipped dog and slink out of the place. I stood tall and never looked back. I took the pain and stuffed it so deep that it would never see the light of day.

A few days later, my buddies and I pulled to a stop in front of my sister's house. Rene threw open the front door and pulled me into her arms. At five-foot-nine, she was a black-haired, dark-eyed beauty, and the only member of my family who loved me.

"Hey, StevieRay!" her husband George said, pulling me into the house and welcoming my friends. "It's so good to see you all! Make yourself at home!" They'd bought an older home, which George had remodeled. It was just like them—happy, warm, and welcoming. It was a gathering place for their son and his friends, as well as for me and mine. Rene was eight years younger than I was, and since I'd left home at the tender age of fourteen, we didn't know each other much growing up. We'd reconnected as adults, and she and George always stood by me.

"How were they?" She stood over the stove cooking something that smelled like heaven in a pot. I knew she was asking about how it went with our parents. Unlike me, she and our brother Wayne had great relationships with them.

"About like always."

"I *told* them..."

"Rene, you've got to stop defending me."

Her snapping brown eyes caught mine, and I knew I was wasting my breath. As much as I hated for her to jeopardize her relationship with them by defending me, she wouldn't stop. I wouldn't admit it to anyone, but every time she did it, something soft and warm wound around my heart. It felt like a barn cat curling itself around my leg.

Rene held Thanksgiving dinner at her house that year. Since I would be there, we were surprised when my parents agreed to come. The house smelled like a slice of heaven, and the table was laden with food. I felt choked with emotion that the whole family was together.

Daddy blessed the food and then served up a dish of his particular brand of thanksgiving cheer. "StevieRay, I'm sure you know you're headed to hell," he announced while serving himself a scoop of mashed potatoes.

The room went silent. I lifted my eyes to his but didn't say a word.

"You're worthless," he said, stabbing a piece of turkey.

I sat still and listened.

"You ought to be ashamed of yourself," he declared, working up a good head of steam.

I looked around the table at my family. Rene and George looked enraged. Mama and Wayne looked smug.

A few months later, we were riding in Provo, Utah, when Luann showed up to watch. I'd never had a woman—any woman, much less one like her—pursue me the way she did. When she walked into that rodeo, I felt like the luckiest cowboy on earth. I pulled her into my arms and blurted the words before I could stop myself.

"Marry me, Luann."

Her eyes sparkled like a million diamonds. Throwing her arms around my neck she said, *"Yes!"*

I felt like I'd won the world championship.

She said yes.

"Let's get married right away." I wanted to seal this deal before she reconsidered.

"Hold your horses, Cowboy. We can't get married anytime soon."

My heart dropped like a clown kicked in the teeth. "Why not?"

She nuzzled my neck as she answered. "Because my divorce isn't final."

I knew she'd been married and had two daughters, who were two- and three-years old. She'd filed for divorce before we met. I'd figured things were final.

"Just because we can't get married yet doesn't mean we can't start our life together now," she said. "StevieRay, give up the rodeo life and move in with me! Would you?"

"Yes!"

I held her close and drank in her scent.

I said yes.

I hated giving up rodeos, but I'd known a choice was coming. As hard as it was for me to leave the life I loved and to say goodbye to my friends, I was happier with her than doing what I loved without her. I figured I could do some rodeos on the weekend.

I finished the last of my commitments and threw my bags into my Chevy Silverado pickup and drove to Cucamonga, California. I don't know what I'd been expecting, but when I pulled up at her address, my mouth felt dry as dirt. I looked around her neighborhood of million-dollar homes. Her house was spectacular—two-stories, stone, and sitting on a couple of acres. Horses grazed in the bucolic setting.

I sat in my pickup trying to get up the nerve to go inside. I felt as though I'd been kicked in the head. She had all this...*and wanted me?*

I finally went to the door. Inside, I met two adorable little girls who reminded me of their mother. In the days that followed, Luann not only made me welcome, she cooked for me, and took care of me. It was a whole new experience. Nobody had ever shown me that kind of love.

One evening Luann walked me to the mansion next door and introduced me to her neighbor. Robert was a nice guy, and we hit it off. He owned one of the largest independent oil companies in the United States. He hired me to train his horses. I got to spend my days with horses and my nights with Luann.

I came home from work one afternoon and saw a tan Mercedes sitting next to Luann's in the driveway. I parked my pickup on the street and got out. Three men walked up to me. All three wore suits, Rolex watches, and expensive Italian shoes polished to a high gloss. I'd seen pictures and recognized the man in the lead as Luann's husband. His no-neck buddies moved like The Hulk behind him.

"I'm Frank D'Angelo."

"StevieRay Hansen."

"Gather up your stuff and get out."

I eyed Hulk One and Hulk Two, then focused on Frank. "Naw, I don't think so. She's divorcing you."

"Do you like life?"

I allowed a smile to tug at my lips. "I love life."

"Then you'd better get your stuff and get out."

They turned to leave and then Frank stopped and repeated, "Do it, if you like life."

I watched them leave, then went inside. "Are you all right?" Luann's eyes were wide.

"Of course. I'm not worried about him."

"Good, because he's going to put a lot of pressure on you to leave."

"I've had pressure before."

That night, we climbed into bed and turned out the light. She was silhouetted in moonlight. "I'm not kidding," she said again. "He's going to put a *lot* of pressure on you."

"Funny thing," I said chuckling. "Those guys looked and acted like mobsters."

"They are."

I really wanted her to be kidding, but the look in her eyes, the seriousness of her voice, convinced me this was no joke. "What do you mean?"

"Frank's dad heads the Los Angeles branch of *the family*. They're mobsters, and Frank is next in line."

"So...you're married to the mob?"

"I thought I mentioned that."

2

ALONE AGAIN

I lay awake for hours after Luann fell asleep. I wasn't too worried about Frank and his crew. What were they going to do? Put a hit out on me? I doubted it. But underneath Luann's cool exterior, she seemed uneasy. Maybe a little rattled. She knew him better than anyone, and it seemed as though she'd been trying to warn me about him.

She'd warned that he would put a lot of pressure on me. What kind of pressure?

The next day I stood in the round pen with a new horse I'd started working. His eyes were wide, and his ears twitched backwards. He was scared and skittish. Luann had seemed a lot like that when Frank had left. Or maybe that had been my imagination.

I'd never gotten the impression that theirs had been a love match. More like a merger between two families. From what I understood, Luann had been promised to him by her parents when she'd been just a girl. Something had gone sour enough in their relationship that she'd filed for divorce.

Not that I was judging. I'd been married and struck out too. I met Doris when I was about eighteen at a rodeo in Victorville,

13

California. Buck and I were walking across the dark parking lot one night when we'd heard a woman scream.

I'd stopped to listen and heard her scream again.

"Don't get involved," Buck warned. "Let's go."

"Are you kidding?" I dropped my war bag and bolted across the parking lot, where I saw a man hitting a young woman. Let's just say I applied a little logic to the situation, and he ran away like the coward he was.

"Are you all right?" I asked. The sobbing girl was about my age, a tall blue-eyed blonde with mascara smeared across her face.

"I guess," she said, still shaken.

"What do you want to do?"

"I'm not going back to him, if that's what you're asking."

"Will your folks come and get you?"

"They live north of Los Angeles."

"I'm StevieRay Bumpus," I said. We took her to the bus station and bought her a ticket home. After that, Buck and I traveled to rodeos in Arizona, Texas, Oklahoma, and Nevada. During those trips, Doris and I often talked on the phone.

It was 1973 when we finally made it back to a rodeo in California. Doris and I were both still kids, but we married right away. We stayed with her parents for a while before moving to Buckeye, Arizona. By then I was doing well competing in rodeos, so I bought a sprawling ranch with two houses, cattle, and some horses. It was a nice spread, and I loved going home to it and my pretty wife.

Doris got pregnant right away and gave birth to our son, Jason. It wasn't too long before she was pregnant again. I was so happy I bought her a new car. I came home from the road one day, and no one was home. About that time, one of our neighbors —an older woman—dropped by.

"Do you see anything going on?" she asked. "Because from the time you leave until the time you return, there are usually four or five cars parked there. Your place is party central, and your wife sees three or four different guys. You don't spend enough time at home to realize she's on drugs. She disappears for days at a time, leaving your kid with teenagers."

She turned and marched away, then stopped and looked back at me.

"One more thing before I go."

"Yes, ma'am?"

"You're an idiot."

I felt disoriented. It was as if the axis of the earth had shifted, and I couldn't find the horizon. None of what she said could be true. My wife loved me. She would never do those things.

Would she?

I felt like a robot as I walked in the house and searched the place room by room. I found a bag of dope in one of her drawers. From the time I'd met Doris, she'd been the true north on the compass of my life. Now that compass was spinning out of control.

Was anything in our life together true?

I walked to the pasture where my horse nickered and trotted over to me. I ran my hand over his neck, his side, and his withers. He leaned his head against my shoulder with complete trust. The same way I'd trusted Doris.

Trust was huge to me. I thought about the drugs I'd found in her drawer. The evidence looked damning, but I didn't want to make any assumptions. When I was a kid, nobody in my family knew about ADHD or learning disabilities. When I had trouble focusing and learning and was hyper all the time, my parents decided I must be on drugs. They'd tried me in the court of parental opinion and ruled against me. A judgment that had never been overturned.

When I moved out at age fourteen, I went back to Kentucky to live with my grandparents. I was happy as a tick on a hound dog until my dad called my grandfather and told him that I was on drugs. I saw the fear in my grandparents' eyes and moved out. The truth was that I'd never taken drugs.

Still haven't to this day.

Every molecule of my being remembered that betrayal and injustice. I couldn't – wouldn't – make the same mistake with Doris. I stuffed the drugs back in her drawer.

When Doris and Jason got home a while later, she kissed me and went to the kitchen to start dinner. I dropped into a chair and asked the question that had been burning a hole in my soul all afternoon.

"Doris, are you on drugs?"

When she turned to look at me, her cornflower-colored eyes were shadowed with sadness. She walked to the table and dropped into a chair with a sigh.

"No, but Arlene is, and she's got some of her stash hidden here. I don't know what to do about her."

Arlene was her twin sister, she'd had a drug habit in the past.

"Is there anything going on that I need to know about?" I pressed.

"Yeah." Her shoulders slumped, and she didn't meet my eyes. "I've been drinking and partying a lot. I'm pregnant, and it's got to stop. I promise you, it will stop."

I wrapped her in my arms, grateful that she'd been honest with me.

Doris gave birth to our second son, Justin, and I loved coming home to my little family. Doris had always been a bit erratic, going a week or two at a time without washing dishes. Other times, she'd be on a cleaning jag. But with two babies to care for, it seemed to me that she was having more and more trouble keeping up with the place. I started helping more when I was home.

The thought of going home made the highway ahead of me look like a ribbon of promise. I'd been on the road a while and couldn't wait to get back to my family. Justin was a few months old and changing every day. I'd just reached the edge of town when I looked in the rearview mirror and saw flashing lights behind me. I glanced at the speedometer, but I wasn't speeding. I couldn't imagine what I'd done wrong.

I pulled over, and the sheriff told me to get out of the car.

"What'd I do?"

"Stand on the side of the road."

He opened the door to my pickup and started searching it. "What are you doing?" I asked, angry. He had no cause to search my truck.

"Stay right where you are!" the sheriff shouted. The anger vibrating in his voice made me go still. I had no idea what was going on. I watched as he tore my pickup apart piece by piece. When he didn't find what he was looking for, he stuck his face within an inch of mine.

"This town's not big enough for both of us," he said. "One of us has to leave."

He peeled away in a cloud of dust. What was that all about? I wondered if he suspected I was a courier for Arlene's drugs. I drove home and found Doris feeding the baby. Jason screamed, "Daddy!" I swung him up and played with him while I told Doris what had happened. "Do you know anything about that?"

She shrugged. "I heard the law was getting squirrelly."

A few days later, I ran into our nosy neighbor. The lines on her face looked as deep as crevices after a rainstorm as she squinted against the afternoon sun.

"Look," she said, "your wife is having an affair with the sheriff. His cruiser stays parked at your house while you're out of town."

I reeled like I'd been hit by a bull. At home, the house was a wreck. Every dish in the kitchen was dirty, and the kids were bawling. I looked Doris in the eye. "Neighbor says you're having an affair with the sheriff. Says his cruiser is parked here while I'm gone."

Tears streamed down her face. "I figured you'd find out. I'm so sorry, StevieRay. I love you. If you'll forgive me, I swear it'll never happen again."

The last thing I wanted was to lose another family. I looked at our kids and figured I'd better do whatever it took to keep our marriage together. A few weeks later, I got home from the road and found the house clean, a roast in the oven, and a cake on the counter.

"What are we celebrating?" I asked as Doris wrapped her arms around me.

"The rabbit died," she said with a grin. "We're gonna have another baby!"

The whole time I held her, I wondered if the baby was mine.

I'd let my parents know when Doris and I married, but they weren't interested. What stuck in my craw was that they wanted nothing to do with my boys. Whatever their opinion of me, my kids had never done anything wrong. Still, they didn't want to so much as see them. I swallowed the injustice and worked harder at making my own family work.

***

Our third son, Cody, was the spittin' image of the other two boys. We had three little stair steps, every one of them blue-eyed blondes. Beautiful, sweet kids.

Our happiness was short lived. I came home from the road one day and found all three kids crying and hysterical. Doris was unconscious. I had no idea how long she'd been that way. I rushed her to the hospital and waited to hear from the doctor what had happened to her.

"Your wife overdosed on drugs," the doctor said.

"What?"

"How long has she been using?"

I was shocked speechless. I stared at him and tried to put the pieces together. This woman I'd left at home with my children was an addict? "I knew her twin sister had a drug problem, but not Doris! Will she be all right?"

"She'll survive this time, but she's going to need help getting clean – and staying that way."

I thought about the day my neighbor had told me Doris was on drugs. She'd ended her diatribe saying, "You're an idiot."

No truer words had ever been spoken. In my effort to be fair and withhold judgment, I'd put my head in the sand. All of a sudden, everything made sense, including her erratic behavior.

I had a wife who'd just overdosed on drugs. I had three little boys who needed a parent. The ball was in my court. If my family had a chance in hell of surviving, I had to step up. My first call was to Buck.

I explained what happened and finished with, "I'm not going back on the road."

"We'll miss you, StevieRay."

My second call was to get Doris into therapy.

Then I found us a church. Instead of riding in rodeos on Sundays, I herded my family into the pews. The old hymns like "Amazing Grace" and "How Great Thou Art" were a comfort to me. I figured we needed all the help we could get – especially prayer.

As Doris worked to get off drugs, I took an active role in the care of the boys. To make money, I'd started buying and selling cattle. In addition to feeding the stock and handling the business, I washed dishes, cleaned toilets, and put meals on the table.

I didn't fool myself into thinking that I could wave a magic wand and make the addictions that drove Doris disappear. What I wanted more than anything was for her to know she wasn't alone. In the evenings after we'd gotten the kids to bed, I poured us each a glass of sweet tea. We sat on the porch holding hands. Sometimes she talked about her struggles. Other times, she seemed lost in her thoughts.

When I wrapped my arms around her, she felt fragile. Like a baby bird with bones so soft they could snap. I had no idea if what I was doing would be enough.

But I didn't know what else to do.

With me at home picking up the slack, Doris began spending less time with us. Some days she had an extra counseling session. Other days, she forgot something at the store. There was always something.

"Let's sit on the porch," I said one evening after dinner.

"I've got to run down to the store." She kissed me and left.

I got a teenager to watch the kids and looked for her. She wasn't at the store. I found her in the sheriff's cruiser, wrapped in his arms and lip-locked.

I stared at them for a full minute before they saw me. It was long enough for me to know I'd had enough. We had three great kids, a beautiful ranch with two houses, and a good life. If that didn't satisfy her, there was nothing I could do to fix it.

I pulled up next to the cruiser and rolled down my window. When she looked up at me, I said two words.

"You're leaving."

I drove home and started boxing her belongings. She walked in the door looking like a kid who'd been caught with her hand in the candy jar. "This is best," she said. "You keep the kids."

Cody was still an infant.

I sent her home to her parents and kept the boys. I knew they were better off with me, but they didn't know it. All they knew was that their mother had disappeared. They cried for her. Wailed for her. Begged for her. And it broke my heart.

Doris' mother called one morning. "She misses those kids so much it's eating her alive. If you send them here, I'll make you two promises. I promise they'll be well cared for. And I promise that we'll get her help."

I could have never let them go if I hadn't watched them grieving for their mother. When I packed up my children and took them to her, I felt my heart shatter into a million pieces. There I was alone. Again. Without a family.

I paid child support, and Doris got a place for her and the boys. I arrived to pick them up at eleven one morning and walked inside to find people lying around half drunk in a mess of empty whiskey bottles. In the kitchen, I found an empty refrigerator and empty cupboards. The boys were dirty and hungry. I took care of their short-term needs and then went to court and sued for custody.

We fought over custody for years. In those days, it was rare for a father to get custody of his children. Doris was bitter and angry, and she told the judge that I was on drugs and alcohol. Not only had I never done drugs, but I'd never been able to drink. Three beers made me too sick to function. Doris was a convincing liar; I gave her that. She spun her lies, and the judge bought her stories just like I had. I continued to fight for custody and she continued to win.

I found out later that she'd taken the boys to the post office and shown them pictures of the FBI's Most Wanted List. She told them that I was a criminal and that the FBI was looking for me. The boys believed her, especially Cody, the youngest. When he was older, he called the FBI and said, "My Dad's been wanted by the FBI for years. I want to turn him in."

The FBI explained that I wasn't wanted by the FBI or anyone else.

I'd received one good piece of advice from a friend when Doris and I split. He told me to keep copies of all the child support payments I sent. Every month, I paid by money order from the 7-Eleven and kept copies of all the receipts.

Although I didn't know it at the time, Doris had told authorities that I hadn't paid any child support, and she'd filed for and received welfare. When I found out what was happening, I went to the district attorney's office and dumped a bag of receipts on his desk. I had proof of every payment. The DA was stunned and filed charges against Doris. She might have been a great liar, but she couldn't lie her way out of all those receipts.

The judge sent Doris to the county jail for fraud, and the court released me from paying any further child support payments. But I couldn't stop supporting my children just because their mother was a mess. I continued to send child support. I figured if ever the judge would grant me custody it was now. In spite of what she'd done, she retained custody.

The next time I talked to my parents, I told them I was divorced. *"Divorced!"* my mother screeched. "As if you haven't brought enough shame on us. We're ashamed to call you our son! We're too embarrassed to hold up our heads because of you!"

While I was finalizing the rest of the legal work, I decided to change my name. My grandfather, Audrey T. Hansen, had always loved me and treated me well. I took his name. Instead of StevieRay Bumpass, I was now StevieRay Hansen. No point in embarrassing my folks more than necessary. In truth, I wanted more distance between my parents and me. I wanted to stop the pain, but nothing helped. I couldn't fix it, so I did the only thing I knew to do. I ran from it. For years, I only communicated with them through my sister.

I carried so much guilt. The way I saw it, I must have been a hell child for them to despise me that much.

I went back to the rodeo circuit, pretending to be whole and trying to gain custody of my boys.

Now, finally, I had a woman's love. Luann loved me. She wanted to marry me. To make a family with me. I wouldn't walk away from that. I would take on the whole damn mafia if that was what it took. Frank D'Angelo had no idea who he was messing with.

THE CHOICE

harvest moon hung low in the night sky as I parked my pickup in the driveway. It had been a long day after one of Robert's mares got kicked by another horse. She was doing better, and I wanted nothing more than a hot shower and clean sheets.

I climbed out of my truck and stretched, enjoying the cool breeze. I'd just walked to the front door to go inside when I felt the short hairs on the back of my neck stand at attention.

I wasn't alone.

I hadn't heard anything, but I had the uncanny feeling I was being watched. Having caught the scent of danger, I went still. On alert.

Was it a burglar? A peeping Tom? An animal foraging for food? I had no idea, but I intended to find out.

Just then Frank D'Angelo and his neckless crew stepped out of the shadows, moonlight glinting off his Rolex.

"I told you to pack your things and get out." Frank's voice was soft, chilling.

"I don't take orders from you, D'Angelo."

His eyes looked flat, dead, and dangerous. Snake eyes. "Let me tell you what's going to happen to you if you don't get out."

"Yeah, what's that?"

"You're going to wake up some morning – but you won't be in your own bed. You'll be someplace far away. Staked in the hot sand. Screaming. But no one will hear you. Ever."

I stepped toward him and leaned so close that I could smell the garlic on his breath. "Give it your best shot."

I turned my back on them, unlocked the door, and went inside.

I understood bullies. Catching a scent of fear empowered them. Fear to a bully was like heroin to an addict. They lived for it like a junkie. Always desperate for the next fix.

I refused to give them a hit.

The threats had started out subtle, but each time I refused to run in fear, he got angrier.

Too bad. I'd had an early education in bullies.

I'd been twelve or thirteen when my parents pulled up stakes and left Little Dixie, Kentucky. They plopped us in an ugly stucco house on the wrong side of the tracks in Ontario, California, a city in southern California with lots of Hispanic and Black gangs. There was a large park nearby that I walked through to get to school. My too-short jeans and Southern drawl made me a target for the bullies of any color or creed.

When one person went after me, I made sure to get some licks in. As soon as that happened, the whole gang jumped me. I'd earned an honorary doctorate degree in bullies – the hard way. I was too afraid to go to the bathroom at school.

They beat me every day.

My parents called me a trouble maker, but Dad's brother finally figured out what was going on. He understood the culture and knew it was just a matter of time before one of those gangs killed me. He bought an old car with only one headlight and suggested I disappear. I didn't have a driver's license, but at fourteen, I drove that jalopy all the way back to Kentucky. That was the last time I'd run from a fight.

I might be outmatched against the Mafia, but I wasn't afraid. And that was making Frank D'Angelo crazy. As far as I was concerned, he could slither out from whatever rock he lived under and come after me anytime he wanted to. He just might get bitten. I knew that when he looked me in the eye, he saw a wild glint there. I made sure he did.

When threats didn't work, Frank went after Luann where she was most vulnerable – her children. Before I came on the scene, Luann and Frank had a solid custody agreement. Luann got the kids Monday through Friday. Frank got them on the weekends.

When he couldn't scare me away, Frank took Luann back to court, asking for full custody of the girls. He knew Luann well enough to know that she wouldn't choose me over her children. While his threats against me continued to escalate, he used custody of the children to pressure Luann into getting rid of me.

When that didn't work, Frank kept us tied up in court – with me as the center of attention. Frank's team of lawyers hired a psychologist to evaluate me, then called him to testify.

"He's an uneducated rodeo cowboy with no roots," the psychologist told the court. "A danger to the children."

Our lawyer hired another psychologist to evaluate me. "Salt of the earth," he told the court. "He's stable and grounded. A great guy."

It was like watching a world class tennis match – and every serve cost thousands of dollars. Attorney's fees were eating up all our income. I was thinking about all this, especially thinking about the money, while I worked with Robert's horses one day. He showed up to watch. Leaning against the fence, he struck up a conversation.

"What do you want to do with your life?" he asked.

"I like training your horses."

"I know you do and you're good at it. But Luann is used to

nice things. You're not going to be able to provide them for her by training horses."

"I hadn't thought about it."

"Why don't you go to work for me and let me teach you the oil business?"

"Thanks, but give me a raise and I'll be happy."

"At least think about it."

I promised that I would. That evening I told Luann what Robert had said. She pondered it over dinner. "You know, he's probably right," she said. "You'll cap out." We talked about it late into the night. The next day, I accepted Robert's offer. I said goodbye to the horses and started learning the oil business.

That first day in the office, I looked at the big computer and telex like a cow at a new gate. It was fascinating to watch as the price changed minute by minute. I'd always been hyperactive, and that may have been part of the reason I enjoyed the oil business from that first day. It moved so fast that it kept my mind occupied. My whole life had been a lot like oil prices: in constant flux.

I loved the business.

It not only kept me busy, it helped keep my mind too occupied to think about anything else. The oil business wasn't complicated. It boiled down to this: buy low and sell high. I understood the markets—just seemed to have a head for it. It was getting all the right permits that could be tricky. Robert walked me through it, teaching me every step of the way. While I missed training his horses, I enjoyed the competitive challenge of the oil industry. Robert started me at a great salary, but every penny went toward our attorney's fees.

I was also getting an education in family law. Every time one thing got settled, Frank filed something else. In family court, you could drag things out for years. And that's just what he did. Months faded into a year with no end in sight. Even with my salary and the alimony Luann received, our legal fees ate everything. When they overwhelmed us and we didn't have the money to pay, Robert loaned us enough to bail us out.

I finally understood what Robert had hinted at all along. Frank was using his money to drag me through court until he broke me financially. He came after me with a three-pronged strategy. 1) Use death threats to try and get rid of me 2) threaten Luann with loss of custody to pressure her to get rid of me, and 3) tie us up in court until he ruined us financially.

Finally, the divorce was final and Luann and I married. Any hope that those two things would change his attack proved to be false. Several years passed, but if anything, he seemed more focused on ruining me. Every time we went to court, Luann left with less time with the girls. He whittled it down like a serial killer cutting out her heart.

As the years passed, the pressure took its toll on both of us. The bloom was off the rose as far as our relationship was concerned. While ours was a nice lifestyle, our minds, emotions and finances were under siege.

What had started as a standoff had turned into a war.

In truth, I was furious that Luann hadn't come to a custody agreement and made it stop. I blamed her, at least in part, for the situation, but I wasn't sure that was realistic. I had no idea what all had happened in their marriage, but one thing was clear. Luann *despised* Frank. During their marriage, they'd lived in New York where he'd run a mob family. She'd hated the way he treated her there, hated the way others treated her. He was a violent, brutal man.

I'd spent thirteen years riding rodeos and learned to hyper-focus on winning. As year after year passed with no end in sight, my motives changed. I wasn't so much fighting for Luann.

I wanted to *win*. To beat Frank. Nothing else was acceptable to me; I refused to consider losing.

"You do understand that he might kill us both," Luann told me.

"He'll *never* kill me! And I'll do everything in my power to make sure he doesn't kill you."

I wasn't afraid of Frank and the mob. I didn't have a single fiber of fear.

I was *furious.*

I'd been tied up in a business meeting with Robert all evening. On the way home, I stopped for gas and had just finished when Frank and his buddies surrounded me.

They might take me, I thought, but not before I did everything in my power to rip Frank's head off his shoulders. And not before one of them threw the first punch. I refused to let him provoke me into starting trouble. I figured that if I had to, I'd crush his skull with the nozzle, doing as much damage as possible in seconds, because I was sure I wouldn't get a second chance.

"Nice shirt," Frank said straightening my collar and brushing his fingers over the polished cotton as though removing lint. "It won't be long before all Luann will have to remember you by will be the clothes in your closet."

He turned to one of his men. "Joey, why do you think that's all she'll have left?"

Joey wasn't the brightest bulb on the block, but he was massive. Looked like The Hulk on steroids. "Yeah," Joey said as a smile split his face, making him look like something resembling a carved pumpkin on Halloween. "'Cause there won't be enough of you to piece together. They won't find so much as a lock of your hair."

I shrugged off Frank's hand and stared into his eyes, ready for the first move. The atmosphere was so charged that it felt as though static electricity could cause an explosion. I bided my time, ready to strike. Then, without warning, the men faded into the night, leaving the lingering scent of expensive cologne.

The threats were constant. I never knew where or when he'd show up. I figured the fact that I was married to Luann and went home to her every night was enough to drive him over the edge. It wasn't a long drop.

Even after she'd divorced him and married me, Frank wanted to pull the strings and control her life. He had us tied up like a calf at a rodeo. I tried not to dwell on it, but he used his money and resources to keep us entangled. He was like a python, taking his time to squeeze the life out of us. It didn't seem to matter how much I made, Frank made sure I spent it all on legal fees. It felt like we were in a maze and couldn't find our way out.

When I didn't think things could get any worse, Frank pulled the plug on our finances. He stopped paying alimony. The salary I made in the oil industry was great, but it was no match for the burgeoning legal fees. To me they looked like Mount Everest on a cloudy day -- the peak so high you couldn't see the top. At that point, we'd borrowed $200,000 from Robert.

One morning after a meeting, Robert closed the door to his office and motioned for me to take a seat. "Look," he said, "I want you to know that I'm okay with the money I've loaned you. This isn't about that. I want to talk to you about your situation.

"StevieRay, you've got to face facts. I don't know what you think is going to happen, but Frank isn't going to stop. He's going to keep doing this until he has squeezed every last dime out of you – and you leave. That's what this is all about. He wants to control Luann, and he's using the kids to do it. This train is heading in only one direction. A choice. He's going to keep putting the squeeze on you until Luann has to choose between you and her children.

"Do you hear what I'm telling you? This isn't going to go away. It won't stop until you're out of the picture. He's going to continue upping the ante until you're out of the game. He's enjoying every minute of this. He won't stop. *Ever.*"

My mind had been circling the situation, but I'd stopped short of admitting that bottom line. Robert's words left me chilled. I knew one thing for sure. Frank was ruining us financially – and using the legal system to do it.

Where could we turn for help?

I told Luann everything Robert had said, and we talked for hours. It didn't matter how we looked at the situation, we couldn't see a solution. The thing neither of us considered, even for a moment, was letting Frank win. That was out of the question.

I would never concede. Pressure might turn coal into diamonds, but it had turned me cold as ice.

"Well, one thing we know for sure," Luann said. "We can't keep up with these legal fees. They're ruining us. Do you think if we ran away and kept to ourselves we could hide from him?"

"Maybe," I said. "Let me do some checking."

We talked about taking the girls, moving to Texas, and living off the grid.

I called some lawyers in Texas and told them what we were considering. None of them thought it was a good idea. The first one said, "Don't do it! He'll get an order, and Texas won't be able to ignore it. It'll get ugly!"

"It might work," the second lawyer said. "Maybe if we work it right and filed from here in Texas, it might give them trouble. At least slow them down."

Taking those kids out of the state was a direct violation of the court order. If we did it, we'd be hunted by the law and by the mob. We'd be on the run for the rest of our lives.

But it would get us out from under his thumb.

4

ON THE RUN

Luann crept into the girls' room to check on them while I turned off the lights and made sure the doors were locked. Then I dropped into my favorite chair and let out a long sigh. My mind was swimming. I looked around the house, stunned that Luann was willing to give it up and the life-style that went with it. She would be giving up her family and all of her friends.

I would like to have believed that she was doing it because she loved me so much she couldn't live without me. She did prefer me, and she loved me in her own way. But the driving force behind this decision had less to do with me and more to do with her hatred of Frank.

Over the next few days as we formed our plan, we decided that if we went to Texas, we'd make a new life for ourselves in the deep south. I'd been there a number of times and liked the area around Corpus Christi. We chose the town of Victoria, which was within a two-hour drive of Houston, San Antonio, and Austin, and close to Corpus Christi. Located on the coastal plains, it was about 50 miles from the Gulf of Mexico and 20 miles from the nearest bay. It sat just east of the Guadalupe River in an area that's considered subtropical.

We chose a time to leave when we knew Frank wouldn't miss us for three weeks. Packing didn't take long, since all we could take was what would fit in my pickup. We didn't tell anyone we were leaving, not even Robert. The only exception was my sister, Rene. She'd proven her steadfast faithfulness to me for years, and I couldn't just disappear without a word. I gave her a number to reach me in case of an emergency.

When we pulled out of the driveway one beautiful, sunny morning, no one suspected a thing. The trip to Victoria was uneventful. When we arrived, I rented somewhere between thirty and forty acres with a new double-wide mobile home on the property. We'd brought all the cash we could get our hands on, and I used part of it to buy cattle. I bought and sold cattle to earn a living.

Although we were busy settling into our new place and starting over, we counted down the days until Frank was scheduled to get the girls. While we stayed to ourselves, always looking over our shoulders, we were almost giddy with relief to be out from under the constant pressure.

It wasn't Southern California, but the land was green with rolling hills. I left when I needed to buy or sell cattle, and we went to town for groceries and supplies. Otherwise, we kept to ourselves.

Although Luann had led a privileged life, she transitioned into country living in a mobile home pretty well. She and the girls helped with chores, and we soon settled into a routine. I'd always loved children, and Luann's daughters were no exception. We had a great relationship. They were too young to know what was going on; they just thought we were on a wonderful vacation. They romped and played without a care in the world. During the day, they climbed fences and jumped in the hay. We listened to the lowing of cattle, chirping insects, and the occasional late night singing of a coyote.

Frank was always in the back of our minds. We wondered what kind of rage he'd flown into when he realized we were gone. We couldn't help but wonder if he'd caught our scent. We watched every car or truck that came near. We kept a watchful eye on our surroundings, on people and in the rearview mirror.

Constant watchfulness was like a program that always kept running in the background, night or day. Aside from that, our lives were peaceful. There was something restful about the land and the sound of katydids in the afternoon. Our phone seldom rang. When it did, it was someone calling about cattle. There was no rush-hour traffic. No schedule filled with a dozen places to go.

A simple life.

Months passed with no connection to our past. There were none of the usual calls from Luann's parents wanting to see the girls or inviting us to dinner. Our family and friends were collateral damage that we felt bad about. Mind you, not bad enough to contact them, giving Frank even a glimmer of our location.

In retrospect, I realize that those peaceful days were like the surface waters with a tsunami swelling out of sight. I didn't think like a criminal, so I never imagined what Frank might do when he couldn't find any trace of us. While we watched the sunset and the girls chased lightening bugs, we had no way of knowing the plan he'd hatched.

He'd kidnapped my brother.

Back in California, D'Angelo and his crew had parked out in front of Wayne's house and snatched him. They terrorized him, threatening to kill him if he didn't reveal our location. Poor Wayne had no idea where we were. Once they knew there was nothing else to get out of him, they let him go, with promises of what they'd do if the situation wasn't resolved soon.

Wayne went to the one person he figured knew where we were. Rene.

Rene, realizing this was an emergency, gave Wayne my number.

I was stunned when I heard his voice. More so to learn that he'd been kidnapped.

"They're going to kill you," Wayne shouted into the phone.

"They're not going to kill me."

"Not just you." Wayne paused, collected a deep breath. They're going to kill all of us."

My brother's words sent chills up my spine. "It's not going to happen."

Wayne's voice trembled with suppressed fury. "They know where we live. All of your family. And they'll kill us one by one until this is resolved."

"Calm down, they're not going to kill anyone."

"Are you *out of your mind?* Where are you?"

"Victoria, Texas."

"I'm catching a flight. We've got to talk about this face to face so that I know you're listening."

Wayne jumped on a plane and flew to Corpus Christi, and I drove to the airport to pick him up. My brother had been terrorized, and I needed to do what I could for him.

I waved when I saw him. He looked pale, shaken.

"I feel like they're watching me."

Walking to my truck, I, too, had the sense that we were being watched. We climbed inside, and I took off. If someone had followed him, I wanted to lose them. The last thing I wanted was for them to follow me home.

The road between Corpus Christi and Victoria was desolate of other traffic, just green rolling hills. Wayne turned and looked back.

"There's a car following us."

I sped up, but so did the other car.

When it got close enough to identify, I noted that it was a dark gray SUV.

Each time I accelerated, so did the SUV.

It stayed right on my bumper. I didn't know how I was going to ditch them, but I had no intention of leading them to Luann and the girls.

I wanted to think that this was just a coincidence. Another car on a lone road. Except every hair on my body stood at attention. My adrenaline was rushing, but I wasn't afraid.

I was angry, and I had one thing on my mind.

Winning.

We approached a steep hill, and I had to slow down. When I did, the SUV pulled up next to us. I looked over and recognized four of Frank's no-neck goons – with guns.

"They're gonna kill us!" Wayne shouted.

I pulled out my gun, ready to take out as many as I could as fast as possible.

Just then, an 18-wheeler topped the hill.

It happened so fast I never got a round off.

That eighteen-wheeler plowed into them head-on while I breezed past.

Looking in my rearview mirror, I saw car parts everywhere.

"Stop! Turnaround!" Wayne, screamed.

"No!" I put as much distance between us and the wreck as possible.

I knew Wayne wanted to stop and see if the truck driver needed help. I didn't want to be anywhere near those men. If the eighteen-wheeler hadn't gotten them first, I would have started shooting.

Four men, injured or dead. Maybe the truck driver, too. I should have felt grief or horror, but what coursed through my veins was relief. We were safe, and I hadn't been forced to shoot anybody.

The last thing I wanted to do was walk up to that wreckage and have one of the survivors shoot us. As far as I was concerned, we'd been given a reprieve. I wasn't going to give them time to regroup and find us. They were too close already.

When my truck screeched to a stop outside our home, I jumped out and ran to Luann.

"They're here."

She caught my look and went into action. "We've got to get out fast."

While she packed, I drove Wayne back to the airport and bought him a ticket home. I figured it was the least I could do. Before he got out of the truck, he let me know we were done. He wanted nothing else to do with me.

As far as he was concerned, I was everything my parents had predicted I would become.

I heard on the radio that there had been fatalities in that wreck. They didn't say how many had died. I never heard. Having seen the wreck, I thought there was a better than average chance that no one survived. I hoped against hope that Frank D'Angelo was dead and this nightmare would be over.

When I got home, Luann and I took care of all our last-minute business, and I made arrangements for someone to get my cattle. Then we climbed into the truck and headed for Battle Mountain, Nevada, where Luann's uncle owned a ranch.

We were stunned at how close they'd come.

We were tired and bedraggled by the time we reached Battle Mountain. As soon as we stepped out of the car, Luann's uncle ran out the door. "There's a warrant out for your arrest. I don't know who died in that wreck, but Frank D'Angelo is alive and coming after you. This has got to stop! We're going to take Luann and the girls back home. StevieRay, you do whatever."

"Not going to happen." Luann turned to me. "I'm staying with you."

The bloom might have been off the rose, but I was grateful that she chose me. After a rest, we took the girls and climbed back into the truck.

Then we headed back to Texas.

5

THEN THERE WERE FOUR

Sun glinted off the highway ahead of us on the long drive from Nevada back to Texas. I figured the last place they'd expect us to go was back there. We couldn't go back to Victoria to get anything, so I leaned on everybody I knew for money. Even friends from our old neighborhood helped us put together enough money to start over.

We chose a different part of South Texas, but this time we lived under new identities. Careful to never use our real names on anything, we rented about twenty-five acres with a mobile home. We started over without so much as a box of salt. We had nothing except what we'd thrown into a few suitcases.

Having almost been caught, we moved with even more caution as I started back in the cattle business. It took a while for us to rebuild our life and for things to settle down. Careful and wary, we soon settled into a rhythm. I knew I could've made money fast on the rodeo circuit, but I suspected there was somebody looking for me at every rodeo in the country.

The girls grew and blossomed under the Texas sun, and when Luann realized she was pregnant, I was thrilled. A child of our own seemed to seal our new life. Our roots settled deeper into the rich Texas soil. My cattle business grew, and as months passed with no warning signs, we got comfortable. Secure in our new identities, we even made friends and socialized with a few couples.

With each passing day, Luann got bigger. Since the business was going well and with the baby on the way, she bought new furniture for the house, which now seemed warm and inviting. I watched her nesting, getting everything ready for the baby.

It had been almost a year since we'd resettled in Texas. I pulled my livestock trailer behind my pickup as I drove onto the ranch of one of my friends one afternoon. The first thing I noticed was a rental car parked there. It was unusual to see rental cars out in the middle of nowhere, and I wondered who he had visiting. I noticed him standing in front of the barn talking to two men.

I parked and was walking toward them when I saw the expression on my friend's face. It sent up flares of warning. I stopped and looked at the two men beside him.

They were D'Angelo's goons.

I bent over and picked up a sturdy branch. I'd bash their heads in if I had to.

"Are you kidding?" one of the men said with a chuckle. "You're not going to do anything with that stick! Now, get in the car!"

"No." I ran toward my truck.

While the men were distracted, my friend slipped inside to get a gun.

I made it to my truck and peeled out, burning rubber, before they could grab me. They ran to their car, and the chase was on. As a general rule, I don't recommend a high-speed chase pulling a trailer, but in this case, I had no alternative. It was hard to outrun a car while pulling thousands of pounds, but I was desperate. It took an hour, but I finally lost them.

I blew up a cloud of dust all the way home. Running inside I said, "They found us!"

Once again, we threw some things in a suitcase and left. Luann gave one wistful look at her new furniture and the baby bed before hurrying the girls to the truck. She was so great with child, she lumbered to climb inside.

My primary goal was to get us out of the area as soon as possible. We headed north and had made it to Dallas when Luann went into labor. I headed for the nearest hospital.

The girls jumped up and down in front of the nursery window squealing with delight at the twins. *Twins!* A boy and a girl, Austin and Crystal. They were stunning, beyond my wildest dreams.

While Luann was in the hospital, we planned our next move. We needed to get somewhere safe where Luann could rest and recuperate. Someplace where the family could settle down and enjoy the twins. I thought about my rodeo buddy, Buck Tally. Buck had been with me the day I met Luann. We'd kept in touch, and he lived on a ranch outside Meridian, Idaho, just south of Boise. I called him and explained our situation.

"Come on," he said.

Now on the run with four children, we traveled as fast as the babies allowed. The girls were beside themselves and helped all they could. We made it to Buck's ranch, and he made us all feel at home. Luann relaxed and enjoyed her babies. The girls exploded with excitement over another new adventure.

Buck and I had another friend whose father owned the sale yard where cattle were gathered for auction. All in all, it seemed like it might be a place to consider settling.

The babies grew, the girls explored, and Luann and I tried to figure out how we were going to start over again with nothing. I enjoyed catching up with Buck and helping him on the ranch.

After lunch one afternoon, we were all visiting when, without warning, six officers from the sheriff's department burst through the door with guns drawn. Even if we'd had a chance, it's hard to run fast with newborn babies.

Luann and I were handcuffed at gunpoint. We watched in horror as they took custody of the girls. My heart twisted as they took them away, screaming for their mother.

Before being locked into separate cells, Luann and I were given two minutes together. She looked devastated, her eyes haunted. In a matter of minutes, she seemed to have collapsed into herself. Then they took her away.

The next day we were led before the judge. "You don't have to agree to being extradited back to California," he explained, "but they'll get you there either way."

I looked at Luann. She was white as smoke and bawling her eyes out. They let us confer.

"What are we going to do?" Luann asked, her sunken eyes like coal.

"I have no idea," I admitted, "but somehow, it's going to be all right."

When they led me back to my cell, I asked to make a call. I phoned Robert and told him our situation.

We agreed to the extradition to California. Handcuffed and wearing orange jump suits, we were flown to San Bernardino. When we arrived at the county jail, Luann's parents had already arranged her bail.

Not mine.

I sat in a small, dank cell with half a dozen other men, chewing my lip.

It was a scary place.

By the time Robert bonded me out, Luann was long gone. Her parents had taken her home, a five-and-a-half-hour drive. I intended to go after her.

"Don't go!" the bail bondsman said. "You're already in a lot of trouble. I need you to tell me that you'll show up for your hearing."

"I'll be there."

The next morning, I rang the doorbell at Luann's parents' house.

"What the hell are you doing here?"

Luann's mother's reaction was no surprise. She'd disliked me before I ran away with her daughter and grandchildren. She despised me now.

"Let him in!" Luann ordered. "Never talk to him that way again."

We drove back to Southern California to meet with Robert.

"I love you both," Robert said when we arrived, "but you can't keep breaking the law. It's got to stop. StevieRay, for now, you need to leave Luann up north with her parents. You stay here and go to work, and I'll get you an attorney."

We agreed to follow his advice. I worked Monday through Friday and then drove to visit Luann and the twins each weekend.

I knew Robert had hired me one of the best lawyers money could buy. Still, I didn't see how anyone could keep me out of prison. As far as I could tell, I'd played my last *Get Out of Jail Free* card. I was going to prison, and was as nervous as a mare in labor. So nervous, I kept calling my lawyer.

He didn't have much to say except, "Stop worrying. And stop calling me."

Easier said than done. I continued to call. Finally, one day he said, "Listen, I've got a buddy. He's got it taken care of."

I didn't know what he meant, but it didn't calm my nerves. I didn't see any way out of the situation. We knew what we were doing when we ran. We were guilty, and we had no defense.

The district attorney agreed to my attorney's request for a trial by judge. I figured he didn't want to put me in front of a jury of parents whose worst nightmare was someone running off with their kids.

Our court date finally arrived. When Luann and I walked into the courtroom, the judge said, "Mr. and Mrs. Hansen, how're you doing?"

He smiled at us.

The district attorney argued his case. It was well planned and well delivered. The worst part was that every word of it was the absolute truth. By the time he'd finished, I'd kissed my freedom goodbye. It was like watching my life get flushed down the drain.

When it was time for the defense, my attorney called the district attorney to the witness stand. Everyone in the courtroom was aghast. For forty-five minutes, my attorney discredited him, piece by piece.

When he finished, the judge threw the case out of court!

I felt dizzy with relief. My attorney smiled and shook hands with Luann and me. When we stepped outside the courthouse, he stopped and turned to us with a furious glare.

"Straighten up your freaking lives! Because you don't *ever* want to go before a judge in San Bernardino County again!" Then he walked away.

The trial had been rigged. I know now that it's called Judge Power.

The attorney who handled my case is now a federal judge.

6

THE ANSWER TO EVERYTHING

I bought a pretty little ranch near Chino, California, and continued working in the oil business with Robert. D'Angelo still wanted Luann back. Maybe he thought that control, manipulation, and terror tactics were romantic. I had no idea. I couldn't figure out how he thought anything he was doing would endear himself to her. Of course, we were back in court over custody. Just like before, we hired three lawyers and a psychologist to try and keep up with all their pleadings and posturing. Once again, he made sure we were broke.

Meanwhile, the threats on my life were more detailed and more frequent. Frank had spent a bundle of money tracking us down, and yet, there I was, a free man. He was so furious, he reminded me of an active land mine, ready to explode with the slightest pressure.

Arriving home from work one day, I found the lane to our ranch blocked. *D'Angelo.* He looked rabid.

"Your days on earth are numbered," he fumed. I tuned out the rest of his diatribe, just letting him finish. I suspected that it was all a bluff. After all, if anything happened to me, everyone would blame Frank.

Still, I was pretty sure those had been bullets—not bluffs—in the guns his goons pulled on Wayne and me. Either way, I was weary of the whole thing.

After all we'd been through, nothing had changed.

"Let's move away from Frank," I suggested to Luann. "Let him have custody, and you can take the girls for two months in the summer."

"Not a chance."

D'Angelo refused to put his kids on a plane and Luann refused to move out of the state. Like it or not, I was stuck in California as the prime target in their ongoing war.

I finally understood what Robert had been telling me for years. Unless I started making money – big money – we couldn't go on. The only other option was for me to walk out on my family. That wasn't going to happen.

Money had never been a big priority in my life. More important to me than money was getting to live the life I loved. That's why I'd been so happy riding rodeos. Back then, all I needed was the money to get from one rodeo to the next. Once I married Doris, I was satisfied with a little spread, horses, cattle, a nice car for Doris, and a good pickup for me. As far as I was concerned, I was in tall cotton.

That was then; this was now. If Luann and Frank refused to settle on a custody agreement, I needed money. Lots and lots of money.

For the first time in my life, money consumed my thoughts. Money was the first thing I thought of when I woke in the morning. It was the last thing on my mind at night. Even while doing my job or playing with my children, it ran in the background. I wrestled night and day trying to think of a way to get enough money to keep up the fight. I twisted and turned the facts like a Rubik's cube I didn't know how to solve.

In spite of Robert's generosity, working for him wouldn't be enough. The bald truth was that if we were going to survive those legal fees, I needed more money than he could pay me.

I needed to be as rich as Robert.

That one thought put all the pieces of the puzzle together.

I had to own my own oil company.

In addition to our money issues, Luann was pregnant again, hormonal and unhappy that she'd gotten pregnant while the twins were still infants. A few months later, I walked into the kitchen and noticed that she looked stunned. "What's wrong?"

"I went to the doctor today," she said.

I froze, hoping nothing was wrong with the baby. "What'd they say?"

"We're having another set of twins."

I looked at Crystal and Austin crawling around making a racket and a mess, and all I could do was laugh. They were beautiful tow-headed children, and I hoped the next two would be just like them.

If there had been any question about the need to start my own company, another set of twins settled the issue. In addition to overwhelming legal fees, we would soon have a total of six kids.

Although I couldn't move my family out of state, I decided that I had to put some distance between us and Frank. I sold our ranch and borrowed enough money to move to Bakersfield, where I started Hanco Oil.

In Bakersfield, I bought a ranch and a tanker. I rented a nice office space, and several refineries gave me a line of credit. Robert connected me with Good Sense Oil, and I bought their refined product and sold it to a conglomerate of Quick Stops.

It had been one thing to work for an oil tycoon. Running my own company was a different situation. Everything happening in the Middle East was reflected in the price of oil, so I became a news junkie, watching eight screens in my office with multiple remotes. I knew every politician and where each stood, every sheikh, and all the players in OPEC. I memorized all the area codes for all the pipelines and gas terminals to help me keep up with my oil. I kept up with my business associates by area codes.

Hanco Oil cash flowed in 30 days.

I made $500,000 the first month.

For the first time since I'd climbed on the metaphoric bull ride of my life with Luann and Frank, I felt intense relief. I paid all our business bills – personal bills and legal fees – and had some money left over.

If there had been such a thing as the Pledge of Allegiance to Money, I would have put my hand over my heart and made it right then. Although I didn't realize it on a conscious level until years later, at that moment, I'd internalized a new truth.

Money would solve all life's problems.

My whole motivation about money changed. If money had been a god, I would have fallen to my knees to worship. In a way, that's what I did because I put getting money ahead of everything else in my life.

Meanwhile, Luann gave birth to our second set of twins, another boy and girl, whom we named Michael and Melissa. Having two sets of twins created a lot of chaos, but we loved every moment of it. And the girls were thrilled with the new babies.

Frank, true to form, continued to threaten me. Even with all that money, the majority of it went to lawyers. We paid psychologists an obscene amount of money. We also hired a private investigator. Everyone knew Frank was in the mob and committing all kinds of crimes. The kinds of crimes that would stop him from getting full custody of the girls. We hoped that the investigator would find the proof we needed that we could admit in court. Fighting that custody battle proved to be the most expensive thing I'd ever done – or would do – in my life.

I'd never seen anything like it, but family court was a revolving door. Once an issue was ruled on, families could refile a new petition and it just went on and on, like a rat on a wheel.

Hanco's sales soared from $500,000 to $5,000,000 a month. By the end of our first year in business, our gross sales were $10,000,000 a month. Our cash flow was so mind boggling that I went on a spending spree. I bought 35 show horses and hired a trainer. We stopped flying commercial, leasing private planes to travel. I bought two of every kind of car I wanted, including two Cadillacs that I never drove.

Life, I found, was much easier with money.

In my mind, it was the only thing that would make the world go away.

Although I was convinced that extreme wealth would solve all my problems, it changed me in a way that nothing else had ever done. Instead of becoming calmer and more peaceful because our financial woes were over, it had the opposite effect on me. In addition to being boastful and proud, I was irritable and on edge. I felt like a bundle of nerves wrapped in skin.

There was a bite in the air one Saturday morning as I watched my trainer work with one of the horses. "Mr. Hansen," he said, "I was wondering if you could float me a loan. I've got this situation..."

"If you want money, get it the same way I did!" I snapped.

When a panhandler asked for a dollar I barked, "Get a job!"

In the office, I didn't tolerate excuses. "What do you mean that you haven't got those invoices ready? Whatever I'm paying you is too much! Your incompetence astounds me!" I ranted and raved over everything.

I was convinced that if I had enough money, I wouldn't have to deal with people like D'Angelo. If people gave me a hard time, I put them out of business and never lost a minute's sleep over it. I took advantage of anyone I could just to get more money,

In those days, the early 1980s, if you made a nickel a barrel on oil, you were doing great.

I made 45 cents a barrel.

I did it by buying product for 50 cents a gallon. Then I looked for buyers who weren't paying close attention to the markets, scalping them for a big profit.

It didn't bother me in the least.

I felt bad that Luann had lived in mobile homes, starting over twice with nothing. In an attempt to make it up to her, I hired maids, cooks, and private teachers for our children. I gave her everything money could buy – except for the man she'd married.

I didn't know myself anymore.

Worse, I didn't care to.

7

TUMBLING DOWN

Crystal champagne flutes clinked amid conversation on the terrace of the country club where lights twinkled in the trees. We'd taken Luann's parents to dinner where, following a round of toasts, my mother-in-law slipped her arm around me.

"I'm so proud of you."

I smiled, but in truth, I almost passed out. "That means a lot coming from you," I replied, giving her a quick hug.

I joined the conversation and laughed at good-natured ribbing, but my mind scrambled to make sense of my mother-in-law. She'd despised me for years, and she hadn't been shy about sharing those feelings.

I'd always thought that she would never approve of me because I wasn't Frank. But that hadn't been the case. All it took to win her approval was to be as rich as Midas.

Who knew?

My brother-in-law, an engineer for Mobile, had come to work for me, which helped spread the goodwill. I now had thirty employees working in the office and was making more money than I knew how to spend, although in all honesty, we gave it our best effort.

It had been approximately three years since I'd started my company and during that time I'd never wondered what would happen if the oil bubble burst. Men like Robert, who'd been in the industry for years, had learned to survive through the markets ups and downs. As an owner, this was my first rodeo. Although I understood the business and was good at it, I'd never experienced a major downturn in the price of oil and gas.

When dealing in commodities, the price is in constant flux. Those changes have to be factored into your equation. Had I run the business in a smaller way and been happy with a good living instead of extreme wealth, we would have weathered the coming storm.

But that's not the way I did things.

Which meant that I was unprepared when the market turned. Older and wiser men knew to avoid debt and keep multiple millions of dollars in reserve.

I wasn't older and wiser.

I was young and cocky.

I never saw it coming.

I'd bought massive amounts of inventory – on credit – when the market turned. It only took two or three weeks before I was upside down. I'd built up a huge cash flow, so although I was losing money at warp speed, it was hard to detect.

I felt like I was on a broken elevator in a high rise – free falling so fast my stomach was in my throat.

"Listen," my brother-in-law said, "I've made a huge mistake, and we're in serious trouble. You're not making any money, and you can't continue on this way."

That evening I read an industry magazine which reported that Exxon was floating checks and the attorney general was determined to stop them. Their plan seemed ingenious to me. They had their account receivables on one coast and their account payable on the other. When they paid their bills, there wasn't sufficient funds to cover the checks. With receivables on the opposite coast, it gave them time to get money into the account before the check hit the bank.

Thus, floating checks.

I can do that.

I knew it wasn't a long-term solution but hoped it would buy some time until the market improved. I set up my payables on the east coast and my receivables on the west coast.

It worked.

I got way out there, floating millions of dollars. Then Bank of America started sending my checks back. One morning I got a call from them asking me to come in for a meeting.

I stepped into a plush office, where two of the head honchos awaited me. We shook hands and made small talk for a few minutes before getting down to business. The bank president didn't mince words.

"You're playing the float."

"No." I locked eyes with him. "I'm not."

Everyone in the room knew I was lying.

I left the meeting and called my brother-in-law, telling him what they'd said. "Make this look good," I ordered.

"I'm not cooking your books! If this goes down, you're in big trouble!"

Everything was falling apart. My creditors were getting nervous and asking questions. Now that I finally had the money to keep up with Frank's legal fees, I couldn't just watch it all go down the tube. Hanco was hemorrhaging money, and I couldn't pay my bills. I was desperate.

One Saturday morning, I called my brother-in-law. "Tell me what to do, and *I'll* cook the books."

He heaved a sigh. "I'll do it."

He cooked the books and signed off on them to Bank of America on Monday.

The refineries I worked with were nervous. They cut off my line of credit.

Luann worked in the office and knew what was going on. Through it all, she only asked me one question. "Do you know what you're doing?"

"Yes."

The truth was that I was in over my head.

My bankers told everyone that I was playing the float. The refinery to whom I owed the most money was owned by a Texan named Oscar Wyatt. He didn't waste his time trying to get me to meet with him in Houston. Oscar and his three lawyers came to me.

"Sign over every asset you own to me," Oscar said, "and we'll work through this."

I rejected his kind offer and walked the men to the door.

As they were leaving, Oscar turned and said one last thing.

"I'll put you in jail." With a nod of satisfaction, he walked away.

If I'd known that Oscar Wyatt was personal friends with Saddam Hussein and Muammar Qaddafi, I might have rethought my response. His pals made Frank and his goons look like The Three Stooges.

But I didn't know that Oscar Wyatt was the most feared man in the oil business.

Years later, a Texas magazine would call Oscar Wyatt the real J. R. Ewing, the fictional character in the television series, *Dallas*. Together, he and his fashionista wife were nicknamed Beauty and the Beast. He had President Bush's ear in 1990, urging him not to go to war with Iraq over Kuwait, a case he didn't win. Later, he negotiated the release of hostages held in Baghdad. He attended OPEC meetings in Vienna, Austria.

I was out of my league.

Friends in Bakersfield loaned me money and gave me good

advice for free. "Cut your staff in half and let your ranch go back to the lender."

I cut my staff in half and then went to talk to the rich oilman who'd financed my ranch for me. I offered to give it back to him. "Don't worry about it right now, StevieRay," he said. "Take care of what you're dealing with and we'll see how it goes."

During that time, one dogged police detective made it his life's mission to build a case against me. The next thing I knew, Oscar had gotten the district attorney to press charges of theft by check, grand theft, and fraud.

A year and a half later, Luann and I were arrested and hand-cuffed at home in front of our kids. We watched, helpless to intervene, as they put our children on a bus and took them away. Luann's girls went into the care of their father. Our two sets of twins were given to Luann's mother. The state froze all our accounts.

We'd spent millions of dollars hiring the best attorneys to fight Frank for custody. Now, with no money to hire them for ourselves, we were at the mercy of the public defender.

8

FAMILY REUNION

I heard the guard unlock my cell in solitary confinement. "Let's go," he said. "Your lawyer's here." Wearing an orange jumpsuit, I was handcuffed and led to a dingy little room that was like a palace compared to my four-by-six cell. I'd had plenty of time to think, and I knew what I wanted to tell the public defender right off the bat.

"I'll do twenty years if Luann doesn't serve any time."

"So noted," the attorney said, jotting it down on his tablet.

Although Luann had known what I was doing, the decision had been mine. We'd lost everything, and there were six kids who needed her. I couldn't stand the thought of her doing time.

During multiple trials, I was held in the county jail for 141 days.

When it was all said and done, I was sentenced to five years and seven months at the High Desert State Prison, located in Susanville, California, for writing $600,000 in bad checks. Luann was sentenced to six months.

Before I got shipped out of the county jail, a lifer gave me survival tips.

"Don't get involved with anyone there," he advised. "They're going to come at you from all sides trying to get you to pledge allegiance. Don't do it, regardless of the pressure.

"Don't have anything to do with the Aryan Brotherhood, which is the white group. If you do, they'll tell you to fight the blacks, and you'll be told to kill. Be especially careful of the Hells Angels. They're demons. Don't even mention their name.

"The Mexicans have blue handkerchiefs, and the Hells Angels have red. Nobody in there will warn you, but those are their signals."

I went to prison on June 11, 1985 – my thirty-sixth birthday.

Climbing out of the bus, I saw huge walls with gun towers on every corner. Inside, I was taken to a room, where I kept my mouth shut and listened to their spiel. "Don't buddy up with anyone until you know who they are. And whatever you do, don't borrow anything," we were told.

A guard handed me a blue shirt, kakis pants with holes in the pockets, shoes with holes in them, three pairs of underwear, three pairs of socks, a toothbrush, and a blanket.

I was assigned to level three – where the worst of the worst were housed.

I followed a guard to a quad overshadowed by a tower. The guards held automatic weapons with large magazines. I realized right then that I'd made some horrible mistakes which were going to cost me my life. I stepped through a door onto the quad. There were six guards with guns, but that wasn't what made my insides turn to water.

A thousand inmates milled around the yard. When I stepped through the door, they all stopped and watched me with menacing stares.

My life was over.

A guard shoved me into my assigned cell, and I almost came

unglued. My cellmate was the scariest human being I'd ever seen. Evil radiated from him, making him seem more demon than human. He was tall, well over six feet, with wavy black hair. A handsome face, until you looked into his demonic eyes. Muscular and tattooed from head to foot.

He was a member of Hells Angels and had murdered a whole slew of people.

"Look in my eyes when I speak to you!" he ordered. "Don't look away!"

"Okay." I obeyed. I understood why it was an issue. I felt sure nobody ever wanted to look into those eyes.

"Are you a plant?" he asked.

"No."

"*They* put you in here, didn't they?"

"No."

"You're one of them," he said, nodding his head. He was out of his mind.

"I wrote bad checks."

"No you didn't. You're a plant!" He paced the cell, agitated and building up a head of steam.

When a guard walked past, I almost crawled through the bars. "I need to get moved, or somebody's going to die."

I hadn't been in prison long enough to learn that it wasn't the guards or even the warden who made important day to day decisions regarding inmates. It was a guy called the Shot Caller.

The Shot Caller, as his name implied, was the person who called the shots. A hardened lifetime inmate, the Shot Caller was feared by the guards because he had the power to set off the inmates at any time.

The guard took my request to the Shot Caller.

Meanwhile, I was stuck in a cell with a murderous, demonic man. The sun was going down, and I was terrified out of my mind. He was crazy scary.

"Get him out of there," the Shot Caller ordered. "That guy's nuts."

With the Shot Caller's permission, I could be moved, but the quad was full, and there was no place to put me.

Each quad held anywhere from eight hundred to a thousand men and has one solitary confinement cell. On the second day, after a long, sleepless, and terrifying night, I was moved to solitary confinement. I stepped into the tiny cell with a concrete floor.

Later, when I was being processed back into the main population, a big black counselor met with me. "What are you doing here?"

"I don't know."

"You're on level three. Why were you assigned to level three? And why are you serving so much time for writing bad checks?"

"I don't know."

"Is that all you did? Write bad checks?"

"Yeah, a lot of bad checks. Six hundred grand."

"Still, that's white-collar crime. This doesn't make any sense. I'll see what I can do."

On the third day, I put a card in my pocket, and it fell through. The guard saw it and wrote me up like I'd committed some kind of crime. "You'll have to sit in your cell until you can appear before the committee."

"*Why?*"

"Holes in your pockets." As though that explained everything.

I was confined to my cell for two days while I waited to appear before some committee. I'd always been hyperactive, and not having anything to do was making me crazy. Having a book to read would have been a blessed relief.

"Time to go," the guard said while opening the door to my cell.

Led to a room where a group of people waited, I stood before them as though on trial.

"Why do you have holes in your pockets?"

"That's the way the pants were when they were issued to me."

"Why didn't you check them?"

"I didn't know I was supposed to," I said, bewildered by the question.

"Let me explain something to you. Inmates rip out the pockets so they can play with themselves while talking to female guards."

Oh!

"I didn't know that. Nobody told me, and I was issued these pants in this condition."

A while later, I was released to the yard. I heard the crackle of the loudspeaker, and then my name was called. "Report to the office."

Being called to the office meant one of two things. Either I was in trouble for some other unknown infraction, or I had a visitor.

"Your dad and brother are here to visit," I was told. "Do you want to see them?"

Nothing could have surprised me more. "Yes, I do."

I felt limp with relief. I'd spent my whole life aching for a relationship with my parents. For all of our problems, having family members show support was worth more to me than all the checks I'd floated. I'd always hoped that one day we could resolve our issues. Coming here to show me their support was more than I could have asked for. Walking toward the visiting rooms, I hoped they brought reading material.

I imagined Dad saying, "You made a mistake, but we're here for you. When you get out, we'll help you rebuild your life." I ached with appreciation that they'd come.

Dad and Wayne sat across the table from me. Wayne didn't speak, but Dad laughed.

"I knew I'd see this day! I knew you'd end up in prison! *I knew it! I knew it! I knew it!*"

I felt pain that no Hells Angel could ever inflict.

"Didn't I always say you'd end up in prison?" Dad asked, not waiting for an answer. "Not only are you in prison, just like I predicted, but they told us that you're already in trouble!"

"They issued pants to me with holes in the pockets. I didn't know I was supposed to report it. The problem was that—"

"You've always got an excuse!" Dad cut me off with a dismissive wave.

I stood and took a deep breath. "Okay, I think we'll cut this family reunion short." I'd never spoken back to my father or been disrespectful to him, and I still didn't. But I wasn't going to listen to any more of his mocking.

I turned and walked away.

I wasn't sure if I'd stood up to him a little bit, or if I'd just made another escape. The only thing I knew for sure was that I was through seeking his approval.

9

TOO MUCH TIME TO THINK

I felt like a wounded animal that someone had kicked in the head. Back in my cell, I dropped onto my bed and closed my eyes. Pain throbbed from a place so deep that I couldn't feel it most days. Being in prison had left me feeling vulnerable – a dangerous situation where my family was concerned. My family's arrival had opened emotions that I had locked away.

I thought back to the worst injury I'd suffered riding rodeos. I'd been bucked off, but my boot got stuck in the stirrup, and I couldn't get my foot out. I still remembered the pain and the *snap* of a broken bone. It felt like every nerve in my body was on fire.

This pain was worse.

There was no drug to stop it.

No cast to help it heal.

It continued to fester, the way it had for years.

Nothing on earth hurt like the pain of being rejected by my parents. As a child, I'd been bewildered, the pain debilitating. I assumed that when I grew up, it would disappear. But that didn't happen. It festered like a boil.

Growing up without love made me hard and angry. I couldn't remember a time when I wasn't aware of anger simmering just beneath the surface of my emotions, ready to explode at any time.

I'd spent most of my thirty-six years trying hard not to think or feel.

I'd spent years perfecting the art of being too busy to think. Now, my time and my thoughts were all I had. I wanted to crawl, screaming, out of my own skin. I would have given anything for a book to keep my mind too busy to ponder my pain.

Memories ran rampant.

I was born June 11, 1949, in Henderson, Kentucky, the first child of Johnny and Barbara Bumpus. They were only sixteen and seventeen when they married – children raising children. They grew up, but their parenting skills didn't.

My dad was lean with wavy hair as black as sin, dark eyes, and a handsome face. He had a whole passel of brothers, and every one of them was handsome with black eyes and olive complexions. My mother was slim with brown eyes and sandy-blond hair.

They were a good-looking couple who must have been horrified when I was born with a birth defect known as hypospadias. In the vast majority of males, the urethral opening for urination is found at the end of the penis. Mine opened onto the shaft.

I suffered through thirteen surgeries from age four to age nine, all in an attempt to correct the defect. The surgeries were terrifying, painful, and humiliating. I remembered crying for my mother, not that it did any good. Each time I had surgery, my parents admitted me to the hospital – and then left me alone, not returning until I was discharged.

That wasn't the way you'd expect a Baptist preacher and his wife to act. My younger brother, Wayne, my little sister, Rene, and I were spit-shined and seated on the first or second row of the church three times a week, while Daddy preached about love, kindness, and forgiveness.

We were all sitting at the supper table one day when I was in grade school when Daddy leaned over and stared at me with a strange look on his face. He mumbled something about the mark of the beast. I felt my face flush at the humiliation. Even I knew the mark of the beast was the mark of the devil.

I walked into the kitchen one day to get a drink of water, and my mother screeched, "What are you doing in this kitchen?" There was never a time when I felt welcome at home. By the time I was ten, I knew I wasn't wanted there. It wasn't even a question.

I was in grade school when I realized that what Daddy preached from the pulpit was not what we lived at home. There wasn't any physical abuse other than the occasional backhand, but neither was there any love, kindness, or forgiveness. While they weren't great parents to any of us, they singled me out and treated me far worse.

We weren't allowed to sit on the furniture. We weren't allowed in the kitchen or the living room unless invited. After arriving home from Sunday evening services, we were to put our shoes by the door and go straight to bed.

"Mama, I'm hungry."

"You're not eating! Go to your room and get in bed!"

On long summer days, Mama sent us outside in the morning and didn't let us back in until Daddy got home. We didn't get any food until dinner. Once I made the mistake of telling Daddy that Mama didn't feed us. She said I was lying.

I never remembered being held, comforted, or told I was loved. Instead, Dad always said that I was the problem, although I never understood what I'd done to make them hate me. I didn't know any different so I believed him. Dad's purpose in life seemed to be to strip me of my self-worth and dignity. He was good at his job. I only knew rejection.

There was one exception. In Henderson, where I was born, I enjoyed a safe haven in the home of my maternal grandparents. Pop and Grandma Hansen were the polar opposites of my parents. They were warm and kind, given to smiles and hugs.

They said words like, "I love you." Their big sprawling house was comfortable and inviting. The scent of apple pie or blackberry cobbler wafted through the house. Grandma spent her days in the kitchen, making sure there was always something for a hungry kid to eat. Sometimes I sat in the kitchen talking to her while she cooked, wondering how she and Pop could have raised a child who grew up to be my mother.

Mama's sister, Aunt Kay, told me that she thought Mama and Daddy moved away from Henderson to get away from Pop and Grandma. Maybe they thought we'd get too much kindness and love. They even handed out forgiveness when we needed it. Mama and Daddy getting away from Pop and Grandma was like darkness fleeing in the face of light.

When Daddy accepted a church position in Little Dixie, Kentucky, I missed Pop and Grandma with a vengeance. However, those years were the happiest time of my life. We lived in the country, and there wasn't another house for miles. That's where I fell in love with country life. The small house was modern and pretty. It sported tan siding and porches front and back, and the whole place was tucked under huge shade trees.

To me, it was the most beautiful place on earth. My friends and I jumped fences and rode cows. We fished in the pond and went hunting. Since my buddies had horses, I learned to ride and found myself as comfortable in a saddle as on my own feet. I loved horses, their big soft eyes and their gentle intelligence. Neighboring ranchers sometimes hired us to shoot pigeons.

Hunting, fishing, and riding almost made up for the times Daddy sat me in a chair and preached at me from the Bible for hours on end. "You're good for nothing!" he told me on a regular basis. "You'll end up in prison! Mark my words!"

I did everything in my power to win my parents' approval. Yet, they showed me contempt, treating me like I'd committed the unpardonable sin. Sometimes it seemed as though to them, my existence was unpardonable.

They seemed to like Wayne and Rene.

In retrospect, I think one of their grievances with me might have been the thirteen surgeries. They didn't have insurance, and in those days, creditors beat on your door. The debt from my medical expenses kept creditors crawling all over the place. That may have been what prompted them to pack up and leave Little Dixie.

Daddy wasn't making enough money to keep us going. He resigned his position and left pastoring to others. Mama and Daddy both had siblings in Ontario, California, so they chose to move there. We left what I considered a little slice of heaven and landed in hell.

When we left Little Dixie, my whole life came undone. I had lots of friends in Little Dixie. I also had Pop and Grandma over in Henderson. We moved to a rough part of a city of two million people, and the whole time I was there, I never made a friend.

I had no more started eighth grade than I cut through a park and got jumped by a gang of Mexicans. The whole gang beat me. I stumbled home bruised and bloody.

"You just can't stay out of trouble," Daddy said when he saw me.

"I didn't do anything! A whole bunch of Mexican boys jumped me!"

"Kids don't just go around beating people up without a reason. You brought this on yourself."

I came home from school bruised and bloody every day. They jumped me in the school bathroom so often that I was afraid to use it. If the Mexican gang didn't get me, the black one did. If I'd expected my parents to show compassion or defend me, I would have been disappointed.

That never happened.

They always blamed me.

I hated going to school for fear of getting beaten, but I also had trouble learning to read and write. In addition, I couldn't sit still. Still can't. The principal called my parents in to discuss me. I was sitting in the office waiting when they arrived. Seeing me there, Dad kicked me in the leg as he walked by.

"Your son is a problem," the principal said. "He fights all the time."

"I don't fight. I just get beat up. There's a difference."

Nobody wanted to hear it. Nobody listened to me.

"He's also behind academically. He can't read or write."

Things just kept getting worse and worse for me. I had nowhere to turn, but I knew I had to get out.

Between the black gang and the Hispanic gang, I wasn't sure I would survive. It wasn't a situation conducive to learning. My mother's brother, Uncle Frank, lived nearby. He understood the culture and knew what I was up against. Unlike my parents, he believed me.

"Have you ever used a knife?" Uncle Frank asked.

"No."

He handed me one. "Carry this. When they come after you, pull it out."

My physical education teacher saw the knife and took it away from me. Then he sent me to the office. I had two black eyes and swollen, bruised ears, but nobody seemed to care. The fights were never one on one. The gangs always attacked in a group.

My Southern drawl made me a magnet for beatings. Nobody wanted to be friends with someone targeted by the gangs. It would draw attention to them. Besides, everyone hated my drawl.

At the next school conference, my teacher kept me in the room while she discussed me with my parents. "He's just not a smart kid," she said with a shrug. "You're going to have to accept that. He's not bright."

I carried those words like a splinter in my soul for most of my life.

The beatings continued, and I became so depressed and withdrawn that my dad's brother, Uncle Ray, noticed.

He got me alone outside and asked, "What's wrong?"

I told him what was happening. He realized that my parents weren't going to do anything to help me.

"You've got to go home," he said, meaning Kentucky.

"I wish I could."

When school let out, Uncle Ray hired me to work for him during the summer. I saved all the money I'd earned. School had only been back in session for a week when the gangs started after me again.

Uncle Ray gave me a blue 1949 Ford with fins. He also handed me two hundred dollars and told me to get to Kentucky as soon as possible.

At supper that night, I told my parents. "I'm going back home." I explained that Uncle Ray had given me a car and some cash for the trip.

I was fourteen years old, leaving California for Kentucky. I didn't have a driver's license. I didn't have a map. My car had one headlight taped in place.

My mother was so excited she helped me pack.

I'd never heard the term dysfunctional. All I knew was that I needed to get out of that house and away from my family. Driving away, alone at fourteen, I felt a sense of overwhelming relief, not only that I'd escaped death—that I'd escaped hell.

10

KENTUCKY HOME

I pulled the car seat as close to the steering wheel as it would go. That old Ford jerked and shuddered as I drove away. I had no idea how to get to Kentucky. I just knew it was somewhere to the east. Turning my back on Ontario and all the misery I'd experienced there, I headed that direction. I'd figure out the rest along the way.

Most kids my age would have been afraid to drive just under two thousand miles. Not me. I was afraid to stay. I felt certain I wouldn't survive another school year in Ontario. I would end up dead, and I figured Dad would preach my funeral himself. As the sun glinted off the road ahead, I imagined him taking off his hat and speaking from his heart.

"He was a rotten kid. I reckon he got what he deserved."

I hadn't gone far before I saw roads heading off in every direction and got nervous. At the next truck stop, I pulled in and asked some truckers how to get to Kentucky. They were nice and pointed me in the right direction. When night fell and I got too sleepy to drive, I pulled off the road and slept in the car.

The next day, I heard the *whup whup* of sirens and saw

flashing lights in my rearview mirror. "You only have one head-light, and it's taped on," the officer said.

"Yes, sir."

"Who are you? Where you heading?"

I told him.

"I need to talk to your parents."

"Talk to my grandpa, that's where I'm headed." I gave him Grandpa's name and number.

After talking to Grandpa, he let me go.

I enjoyed driving through Arizona. I saw lots of cowboys and cattle. It reminded me of Little Dixie, only on a larger scale.

I made it all the way to New Mexico before I had a flat tire. I stood next to the car and kicked the tire. It was as flat as roadkill, and I didn't have a spare. The sheriff pulled up and got out of his car. "Where you headed?"

"Henderson, Kentucky."

"You're a long way from home."

"Yes, sir."

"You been sleeping in your car?"

"Yes, sir."

"This town gets rowdy on Friday night. You wouldn't be safe out here. Get in my car, and I'll take you to town."

He drove me into town and checked me into a hotel. Handing me the key he said, "Don't leave. I'll be here in the morning."

Sure enough, the next morning he took me to breakfast and then to my car. He'd had my flat fixed overnight. Never asked for a penny, just sent me on my way.

After driving 1,974 miles, nothing ever looked so good to me as my grandparents' house. Grandpa was six-four with sandy blond hair. A deacon in the Southern Baptist Church, he was the kindest man I'd ever known. He wrapped me in a bear hug and welcomed me home. Grandma told me she loved me and put a hot plate of food on the table. Their youngest daughter, my Aunt Kay, was only eight years older than me and lived at home.

"You going back to school?"

"No." I'd already been told I wasn't bright. Didn't see any future in going back.

"What're you going to do?"

"Find a job."

"You can work for me," Grandpa said.

Grandpa specialized in building and remodeling churches all over Kentucky and Indiana. I was thrilled to work for him. I got paid, and there was no fighting. Even better, there was no strife or upset at home. It was a wonderful life. I was happy for the first time since we'd left Little Dixie. Everything was great until my dad stuck his oar in the water and messed things up.

My parents had written me off as bad seed. They never called to talk to me. Never even asked how I was doing. Instead, Dad called Grandpa and convinced him that I was jittery and didn't sleep much because I was on drugs. Grandpa sat me down for a talk.

"Son, are you on drugs? You need to tell me."

"No, sir."

My dad had turned Grandpa against me. Destroyed my new family life. It felt like he couldn't stand for me to have any kind of happiness.

I didn't know it at the time, but I was dyslexic and had attention deficit disorder and hyperactivity. I couldn't sit still. Once a week either my grandpa or my uncle sat me down to talk about drugs. Aunt Kay believed me that I'd never taken any drugs. My grandparents let me stay, but my father had muddied the water.

I could tell they were afraid of me.

I couldn't stand seeing the fear in their eyes. With each passing day, I felt more like my emotional boat was overloaded and starting to sink.

The sky was pewter and icicles hung from trees, glistening like ornaments as I drove to work one morning. The road was slick, and when I pressed the brake to stop, nothing happened.

My 1949 Ford slid into the back of another car. No one was hurt, but I didn't have insurance.

I figured it was time for me to leave.

By now I was sixteen and had a Kentucky driver's license. Pondering where to go, I remembered how much I'd liked Arizona. I saved a few paychecks and told my family goodbye, certain they would sleep better when I'd gone. In addition to going to Arizona, I had one goal in mind. Years before, I'd seen a rodeo and decided that was what I wanted to do. I wanted to become a rodeo cowboy.

Once I got to Arizona, I bought a newspaper and circled apartments for rent. One man had six or seven little bungalows on sixteen acres. It sounded perfect for me. When I arrived, the manager walked outside. I must have been a sight. I was a kid driving a car as old as I was with one headlight taped to the front.

"You have a place to rent?" I asked.

"I do."

"I want to rent it."

"Do you have money?"

"I don't have a job yet."

"Where you gonna work?"

"A feedlot. You'll have to wait on the first and last month's rent until I get paid."

I have no idea why, but he let me move in. He had horses, and I agreed to take care of them for him. Being around horses again made me happy.

I settled into a little two-bedroom apartment and lived on peanut butter and jelly. I found work at a feedlot, a big outfit owned by Mormons in Utah. For the next two years, I made a lot of friends among the cowboys, including Buck.

I was about eighteen when I left Arizona to ride the rodeo circuit. I'd left school not knowing how to read, but it was while riding rodeos that I decided to teach myself. We'd stopped to buy coffee and Twinkies one day when I saw a copy *The Wall Street*

Journal in the news rack. With everything in me, I wanted to be able to read and understand the financial pages. I threw a copy onto the counter.

"What're you doing?" Buck asked.

"I want to read the financial pages," I said.

During our next stop, I bought a pocket dictionary and began the tedious process of looking up the words I didn't understand in the newspaper. I did the same thing with the Bible. That was how I learned to read: from the Bible and *The Wall Street Journal* while traveling the rodeo circuit.

I loved everything about rodeo life, but my parents couldn't understand living on the road most of the time. No matter where we rode, I always found a church. I liked black churches best. I learned to love black gospel music and listened to Aretha Franklin and Elvis Presley in my truck.

My parents considered being a cowboy a waste of time. Especially my dad. He didn't approve of my career or the way I dressed. Of course, he didn't approve of much of anything where I was concerned. But then, the rodeo circuit was where I met Doris. And Luann—and ended up in prison.

My father's predictions seemed almost prophetic.

11

PRISON YARD

I smelled the musty scent of fear mixed with body odor, bad
breath, and something so nasty I couldn't identify it that
first day as I stepped out onto the prison yard. Surrounded
by some of the meanest men on earth, I wished more than
anything to be invisible, unnoticed.

"Hey, Handsome! Where you going?" A man almost as terrifying as my first Hells Angel put out a hand to stop me.

I played dumb and kept walking.

Stepping into a crowd of that many criminals shoved together
in a small space felt like stepping into a nuclear reactor. Anything
could spark an explosion. My first day on the yard, I made a
heart-cry to God. I knew it would take a miracle to get me out of
this alive and unscathed.

I could meet my maker any moment of any day, and I needed
to prepare myself for that encounter. The problem was that it
took constant awareness and watching to stay alive. Any moment
that my mind wandered might be my last.

I existed in full-blown survival mode.

My third day in the yard, two Mexican gangs got in a fight
right in front of me. I kept my eyes straight ahead and kept

walking while they stabbed one another, turning it into a blood-bath. I made it to the other side of the yard in full-blown panic, splattered with blood.

It felt as though I'd grown up and been thrown back in Ontario among gangs on steroids. Only this time there was no escape. Trembling in my cell that night, I wondered if any of the boys who'd beat me bloody as a kid were here filing down shanks and stabbing people. A shudder shook my body. I wouldn't doubt it for a moment.

Murder in prison wasn't like murder on the outside. If you killed someone inside, you didn't go back to court for a trial. You went before a committee. The maximum an inmate got for murder inside was an extra three years attached to their sentence.

"You pledging allegiance to us?" a white guy asked me the next morning on the yard.

"No."

"Why? You're going to need us."

I remembered the advice from the lifer in the county jail and walked away.

On the outside, money was the currency people would kill to get. On the inside, a candy bar was enough. Candy bars, I learned, were a big deal. A powerful currency. If an inmate borrowed a candy bar and didn't pay it back by midnight, one thing was certain.

They were coming for him.

The next time I met with my counselor, he looked at me with sad eyes and shook his head. "I don't understand it," he said. "There are no white-collar criminals in this prison. None. Except you. So I wrote to your judge and asked for a lesser sentence."

"What'd he say?" I asked with a glimmer of hope.

"A resounding no. So, I asked that you be transferred to a different level prison."

"And...?"

"Again, a resounding no. I don't know who hates you, but he has a lot of clout and political power."

I knew who was wielding his power against me. Oscar Wyatt. It wasn't enough that he sent me to prison, he wanted me to suffer. He wanted me scared out of my wits. He'd gotten his wish. I suspected he wanted me to die a horrible death.

"You're stuck here," my counselor continued. "You're going to have to be very particular about who you associate with. Don't leave your cell without your case file. Having the paper with you might save your life."

Two different counselors wrote the judge, but it did no good. There was a guy who'd killed and cut up some kids. He only served six years. I served five years and seven months for bad checks.

Back on the yard, I tried to make myself invisible, but it didn't work. They surrounded me like a pack of hungry wolves.

"We need to know your crime," the leader said.

I knew he wouldn't believe me, so I just handed him my papers. The wolves gathered around and read it over his shoulder.

"He wrote *bad checks!*" the leader said with a smirk on his face. "Leave him alone."

I lost count of how many times those papers saved my life.

One of the inmates had several guitars and played the blues. I loved listening to him play. He saw my interest and offered to teach me. I spent all my free time practicing, playing, and writing music. When he was discharged, he gave me one of his guitars. My Bible and that guitar helped me keep my sanity.

Winter in Northern California hit with a blinding snowstorm. It snowed for four months. On the outside, snow seemed pure, as though it washed away all the filth and grime. Here, it made reality more frightening. Blood splattered on pristine snow like a bright red blossom made my stomach clench in nausea.

I heard my name announced over the speaker system one morning calling me to the office. A rock settled in my stomach as I made my way there. "You're going to work for the warden and me," the lieutenant said. The first job they gave me was to be in charge of bed assignments.

That was a big deal.

There were two men assigned to a cell, and I decided who would bunk where.

I was also assigned to take care of the garden and the livestock. I loved it, because those jobs took me off the yard, which made me feel safe. Still, I got called back to the yard numerous times a day to make new bed assignments.

I stayed busy from the moment my eyes opened in the morning until I crawled into my bed at night. Only when I worked in the garden or with the livestock did I let my mind wander to Luann and the kids. They were my reason to live, the reason I wouldn't let myself fall into despair and give up. My goals were simple. Stay alive, serve my time, and get out in one piece. Fix my marriage and put my family back together.

Months passed, the earth thawed, and I watched tender green shoots spring up from the soil. I'd been in the penitentiary for a year before I got to use the telephone. I called Luann.

"Let me make this clear," she said. "We're not getting back together. I'm going to divorce you. When you get out, you're not going to see me or the kids."

I felt like a rodeo clown who'd just been kicked in the chest by a bull. I staggered out to the garden and began pulling weeds like a madman. I knew it was too dangerous for me in the yard. My emotions were so volatile that if I wasn't careful, I would spark a war.

I sat on my knees in the rich, dark soil panting like I'd run a marathon. I'd wrecked the plants. I used my sleeve to wipe sweat from my face. It wasn't possible that some of the moisture on my face wasn't perspiration, because men in the pen didn't cry.

Not if they wanted to live.

Any sign of weakness drew predators.

I picked up the plants I'd ripped up in a rage and replanted them in a neat row. While I worked, my mind raced with the implications of Luann's words.

Luann had known what I was doing floating checks. I realized now that breaking the law wasn't a problem in her rule book. Getting caught was unforgiveable.

The fact that she was divorcing me was painful. Telling me that I couldn't see the kids was devastating. If it had been anyone else, I might have hoped that she'd relent and let me see them.

I knew without a doubt that she would never change her mind.

Everything we'd been through – leaving our homes, furnishings, my job, our identities, running from the police, and being stalked and shot at by the mob – it had all been about her stubborn refusal to compromise on visitation. We'd known every step of the way that taking those kids out of state was illegal. We'd justified our actions based on what a sorry excuse for a human being D'Angleo was and how he'd used his money and the law against us.

But I wasn't D'Angelo. I'd put my whole life on the line over and over to help her keep her girls. I'd never imagined that she would do worse to me. She didn't plan on letting me see my kids. She didn't want me in their lives.

My only recourse was to hire a high-priced attorney and go to court. I knew what would happen. We would spend years – and millions of dollars – in family court with nothing getting resolved. I would be back in the same mess that had driven me to make money at any cost. There would never be enough. I'd ridden that train right into the penitentiary.

If I got out of prison and chased money like a god again so I could spend it on attorneys, I knew what would happen. The last vestige of humanity would be stripped from my soul. The way I saw it, the decisions I made here in prison would determine what I did for the rest of my life. If I let myself be pulled back on that cash-cow merry-go-round again, I might as well give up and die here.

I sat back on my heels and lifted my tortured face toward the morning sun. I hadn't just lost my freedom. I hadn't just lost my marriage. I hadn't just lost my family.

I'd lost my kids.

I pictured their faces and wanted to howl like a wounded animal.

12

FREE AT LAST

A chill rippled down my spine as I put the prison vehicle into gear and drove toward the guard tower. My mouth felt dry knowing that I was in the crosshairs of several rifles. I stopped at the gate and showed the guard my papers. He inspected the vehicle and then waved me through. A mile from the prison when I could no longer see it in my rearview mirror, muscles that hadn't relaxed since the day I'd been processed sagged in relief.

I felt like pinching myself. The warden trusted me enough to let me drive to town to buy feed and supplies for the livestock.

I parked the truck and went inside the feed store. Small things gave me an unexpected thrill. The *ding* of the bell alerting employees that someone had come inside. A smile and a nod from another customer. A greeting from a salesperson. In another lifetime those moments had been so normal as to be forgettable. I no longer took them for granted.

More than anything I cherished the freedom to make a choice.

A respite from fear.

I drank in the delicious scent of hardwood floors, pine soap, feed, and grain. Music that I hadn't heard in years played in the background. I didn't realize how much I'd missed it.

"How can I help you?" the clerk asked, stepping from behind the counter.

"I have a list of what I need." I handed him a paper.

Too soon, the vehicle was loaded, and I left, taking the long way through town. I stopped at lights and looked in store windows. I watched a student driver careen up and down the street in jerky movements, and I smiled. I watched a father throw a ball to his son. A little girl in pigtails high-stepped in pink rollerblades while a puppy nipped at her heels.

Normal, everyday scenes.

I felt like weeping from the pure joy of it.

The muscles in my shoulders knotted up almost all the way to my ears when the prison came into view. I stopped at the gate, awaiting clearance to take myself back to hell. No matter how long I stayed, I would never get used to life in prison.

Which was why I didn't veer from the warden's instructions. Assigning me to work with the livestock and the garden had given me a reprieve from the yard. Being allowed to leave the prison and run errands in town was more than I had hoped for. No way would I betray that trust.

I spent most of my time with the livestock. Working with them was as restful as I could get on prison property. Bible stories drifted up in my memory. Especially the story of Joseph. Like him, I'd been rejected by my family. Like him, I'd ended up in prison. And like him, I worked for the warden.

I found myself pondering Joseph's life. There were two major differences between my life and his. The main difference was that I had committed the crime that landed me in prison. Joseph had committed none. The other difference was that although we'd both found favor with our jailors, Joseph's story had a happy ending.

I couldn't imagine mine would.

As months faded into years, there wasn't a day on the yard that wasn't fraught with danger. The only places I could let down my guard were with the livestock, in the garden, and sometimes locked in my cell. Those respites forced me to do the thing I'd been running from my whole life.

Think.

My entire adult life, I'd worked hard at staying too busy to think. My mind seemed like my own worst enemy – taking me where I didn't want to go. It kept trying to look at the pain from my family's rejection, trying to make sense of it.

In refusing to think, I'd run from the pain that threatened to overwhelm me.

However, in prison, I couldn't escape my own thoughts. They often floated into my consciousness in verses set to music. I started writing songs, which was a kind of therapy for me, eventually writing over two thousand. After I finished each song, I mailed it to Rene, who got it copyrighted for me.

I'd served half of my sentence when I realized that I knew one thing I wanted to do with my life when I was released. I wanted to start another oil company. I had been good at it, and I'd enjoyed the challenge. Only this time when it made money, I wanted to have the kind of wisdom Joseph had handling wealth. He'd made sure there was enough grain in the storehouses to last through years of famine. God used his position of power to rescue the brothers who'd sold him into slavery.

Could I ever be that generous to my own family? God alone knew the answer to that question.

What I did know was that I would never again live an extravagant lifestyle. When I looked back over my life, I'd been happiest with a simple life. Paradise for me would be living on the wide-open spaces of Texas with gardens, cattle, horses, and the love of a good woman.

As I contemplated reinventing my life, I realized that more than anything, I wanted it to be pleasing to God. I wanted what was left of my life to be built on the foundation of God's Word. I wanted a good church where I could invest myself.

I spent months pondering what I would do with the imaginary money I made in my reinvented life. One afternoon the answer dropped into my consciousness like a coin in a slot machine.

I wanted to help kids like me. Throwaway kids like me who didn't belong anywhere.

I pondered the hypocrisy I'd experienced with my family. The disconnect between what my father taught from the pulpit and how he treated me at home. I figured there must be a way to reject the hypocrisy and live my life in a way that pleased God.

If there was a silver lining to being in prison, it was that my circumstances had caused me to face my own mortality. That revelation had led me to the next one. I wasn't ready to meet God.

I knew *about* God. I knew fire and brimstone. I knew what it felt like to have shame and guilt heaped on my head like coals of fire. What I'd never experienced – and what I ached for – was the love of a Father. I'd never experienced true forgiveness because I'd never experienced true repentance.

It took prison to get me to face the truth.

I needed a Savior.

Locked in my cell, hoeing the garden, or worming livestock, I did business with God. I asked Jesus to be the Lord of my life. I repented of my sins. There was no sudden, blinding light. No transformation of my life like what Paul experienced on the road to Damascus. I was as messed up as I'd ever been. But little by little I was changing on the inside. It happened in increments too tiny to notice.

I stood in the garden among a harvest of fresh vegetables one summer morning. A plump yellow onion felt weighty in my hand. That bitter onion reminded me of my life. I felt as though the Lord was peeling me like that onion. Layer after layer of sin, deception, and trauma were being stripped away.

I didn't know a lot about faith, but as far as I could tell, it meant I needed to trust God to remove the bitterness and make something good out of my life. I had to let go of a lot of things. Most of all, I had to let go of my pride.

I also had to let go of the pain of mail call. I'd never received a single card, letter, phone call, or gift. No news from the outside. Not a single word of encouragement. Not one expression of concern. Not a single visitor except for my father and brother, who'd come to mock me.

Jesus was mocked too. His closest friends denied knowing him. I figured He'd had some experience with rejection and could help me through mine – and He did. What He didn't do was part the waters for me by giving me an early parole. I suspected that God needed the full five years and seven months to get my attention. Once He got it, scales fell off my eyes. I saw with sudden clarity that almost every decision in my life had been motivated by one thing.

Running from the pain of my parents' rejection.

From the time I was a little kid left alone in the hospital for surgery, I'd wondered why they didn't love me. What had I ever done to earn their hatred? Over the years I'd internalized all that pain and let it derail me time and time again.

I knew I had to stop stuffing it deeper. I had to take it out and face down the lie that it had led me to believe.

That I was unlovable.

My family couldn't love someone as unlovable as me. Doris couldn't stay faithful to someone as unlovable as me. Luann found me so unlovable that she had to keep our children away from me.

Alone in the prison of my thoughts, the Lord put his finger on that festering lie and said it wasn't the truth. I understood that He wanted me to stop letting that pain and sense of abandonment and betrayal drive me to unhealthy relationships that sabotaged my life and reinforced that lie.

I had to believe that there was something lovable in me for one simple reason. God so *loved* the world that He gave His only begotten Son. He loved me. Which meant that there had to be *something* lovable in me. I had to let Jesus' love heal me, fill me... and be enough. I'd spent too much of my life like Lot's wife – frozen in place, my eyes on the past.

It was in the fifth year of my prison sentence that the Lord let me see myself in the mirror of His truth. For the first time, I stopped making excuses. I called a whole litany of life choices what they were.

Sin.

I not only admitted that my choices had been wrong, for the first time I took a hard look at what had motivated those decisions. Even my motives had been wrong.

Yes, my parents had made a host of mistakes. Yes, Doris had lived a lifetime of mistakes. Those, I realized, didn't nullify my own. The Lord peeled away layer after layer of self-deception until I stood before Him naked and bare. Without excuse.

I repented to God. Cried out to Him in my distress. That's when I experienced the miracle of a Father's love. Love clothed me in righteousness. Love lifted my head and showered me with kisses of grace.

I may have been imprisoned in one of the toughest maximum security prisons in the nation. But for the first time in my life – I was a free man.

13

ON THE ROAD AGAIN

I thought my heart was going to jackhammer its way out of my chest that blustery spring day in 1991 when I was released from High Desert State Prison. I knew without a doubt that it had been the grace of God that had kept me alive and protected for five years and seven months. As soon as I got out, I talked to a friend from Bakersfield. "StevieRay," he asked, "why is that detective living on your ranch? There's not a policeman alive who could afford it."

"What detective?"

"The one who investigated you."

A creepy feeling crawled up my back like a spider. He was right about one thing. No one living on a policeman's salary could afford that ranch. In addition to a stunning home, it featured an Olympic sized swimming pool, a regulation size tennis court and stables.

I investigated the situation and what I found smelled worse than a pile of manure. When I went to prison, Oscar Wyatt bought my ranch.

Then he gave it to the detective who built the case against me.

If I'd had any doubt that Wyatt had pulled strings to get me arrested and assigned to a maximum-security prison, those questions were settled. I also felt sure he'd been the one blocking my transfer to a different prison. I shook with suppressed fury, knowing full well that there wasn't a thing I could do about it.

I forced myself to put it aside and concentrate on rebuilding my life.

During my prison sentence, I hadn't heard from a single friend or family member except for that one unwelcome visit from my dad and brother.

I was forty-one years old, and as far as I could tell, there wasn't a person on earth who cared about me aside from my sister, Rene, and my grandfather. Those were the two people I most wanted to connect with on the outside. When I called Rene, she welcomed me into her home.

"How's Grandpa?" I asked.

A shadow fell over her beautiful face. "He's gone."

"What?"

"He died while you were in prison."

I had to remind myself that ex-cons didn't cry. At least not until they were alone at night. I hated the fact that I would never be able to hear my grandfather's voice again or get to tell him what God had done for me. He would've loved to hear about it.

None of the counselors wanted me going to a halfway house when I was released since eighty-nine percent of people who do end up back in prison. I would have been forced to go to one if Rene hadn't taken me in. I worked putting on roofs all day. Rene got me a piano and a guitar. At night, I sat in the forty-foot RV in Rene's back yard and wrote a blend of country music and blues.

"What do you know about Wayne being molested by an older boy in Little Dixie?" Rene asked as she started dinner one evening.

"Did someone molest him?" I asked, shocked.

"Yeah." Rene filled me in on the story.

"I remember Mom and Dad dropping us off with that family

for the weekend," I recalled. "I thought the kid was odd, but he never approached me. I knew nothing about what he did to Wayne."

"Wayne told the family about the molestation two weeks before you got out of prison," Rene explained. "That's why Mom and Dad don't want to have anything to do with you now."

"What, they blame me?"

"Yeah, apparently. And so does Wayne. Since you were older, they all expected you to protect him."

"I was just a kid. And Wayne never told me."

I walked outside and took slow, deep breaths. *Here we go again.* The fact that my little brother had been molested was horrifying to me. Even as a kid, I would have done anything in my power to protect him if I'd known. But the elephant in the living room that everyone seemed to ignore was that it was the parents' job to protect the children.

It had been their job to protect me in the hospital during those thirteen surgeries. It had been their job to protect Wayne from molestation. However, they weren't accepting any responsibility for leaving us with that family. Once again, I was cast in the roll of the family villain. The proverbial scapegoat. The whole thing was so twisted and dysfunctional, it made me want to pull my hair out. I couldn't let it get to me.

I decided to address it with Wayne.

"Wayne, I'm sorry that creep molested you. If I'd known what was happening, I would have helped you. I'm sorry I didn't protect you."

Wayne offered me a job, and things rocked along okay for a while. Sometimes he'd get cranky with me for no apparent reason, and I would apologize again. He had trouble letting it go.

Rene helped me get a car, and I drove to meet my parole officer and settled into a chair across from his desk. "What's your plan?" he asked.

"I'm living with my sister and working for my brother," I said, handing him a piece of paper. "Here are their names and addresses."

"Luann and the kids are still living up north," he explained. "She divorced you. If you go see your kids, you'll violate the conditions of your parole and go back to prison."

Luann had warned me that she would fix it so I couldn't see the kids, and I'd had years to deal with it. Still, the finality of the situation felt like a kick in the chest. I'd served the time for my crime. It was cruel to require me to give up my children in order to stay out of prison. That was a life sentence that only a child abuser should suffer.

I'd always heard that the transition from prison to life on the outside could be difficult, although I didn't think it would be for me. I was wrong about that. Since the day I'd left Henderson for Arizona, I'd been on my own and made my own way. Now, in my forties, I found myself dependent on my sister and brother-in-law to put a roof over my head. And on my brother for a job. As I struggled with the feelings that dependence brought out in me, I recognized the root of the problem.

Pride.

Once I realized what it was, I humbled myself with a thankful heart. I knew I needed to find a good church where I could learn more about living for God. Wayne and his wife invited me to theirs, and I was happy to go. Their pastor, a woman who reminded me of a throwback to hippy days, was related to my brother's wife.

I settled into the church, knowing I had a lot to learn. The church was filled with some wonderful people. The proverbial salt of the earth.

Months passed as I kept my head down and stayed out of trouble. While I wasn't happy, I was thrilled to be out of prison and grateful to be alive. I was content. That's why it caught me off guard one Wednesday night when the pastor got in my face.

"You know," she said, "you're a big part of the problem with your family. And with your brother."

"Okay..." I said almost too stunned to speak. I had no idea what this was about or where it was going.

"You need to make all of this right," she continued with eyes blazing.

The confusion I felt must have been visible on my face. "I...I don't understand," I admitted. "What do you mean?"

"Get rid of the costume and get into the real world."

"Costume?" I had no idea what she was talking about.

She waved a dismissive hand at my jeans and boots. "Yeah, the *costume!*"

There weren't many cowboys in California, so I stood out. She didn't seem one to talk, though, considering she dressed like a hippy. Still, I left the church trying to figure out what I'd done to set her off. I didn't have a clue, except I figured it came from my family. No matter how many times I'd apologized, they still hadn't forgiven me.

My mother's younger sister, Aunt Kay, called. Aunt Kay was eight years older than me and had been around my family and me a lot before we moved to California. She'd also been living at home with her parents – my grandparents – when I left Ontario and drove back to Henderson.

"Aunt Kay," I said, "just level with me. Was I a rotten kid? A problem child?"

"Absolutely not. You never caused a minute's problem. You always did whatever anyone asked of you."

That's pretty much the way I remembered things, but I figured I must have forgotten a lot. I knew that I'd never spoken to my parents with disrespect as a child or as an adult. I didn't remember any willful disobedience. My behavior, as far as I remembered, was no better or worse than Wayne's or Rene's. Just kid stuff.

Still, I knew that the Bible says that as much as it is possible, we should be at peace with one another. I'd also learned what Matthew 5:23-24 said. "Therefore if you are offering your gift at the altar and there remember that your brother or sister has something against you, leave your gift there on the altar. First go and be reconciled to them, then come and offer your gifts."

I figured the fact that the pastor got in my face meant that my family still had an offense against me. I called my mother and apologized again. I apologized to Wayne and then Rene. I was still looking for love, but I only got more rejection, except from Rene.

Everyone except Rene gave me the cold shoulder and refused to accept my apology. Rene wrapped her arms around me in a fierce hug. "I never bought into what they said about you."

I'd spent almost six years in prison learning to control the rage that simmered beneath the surface. I still had pockets of anger that spewed up when I least expected it, making me want to hurt someone. One day something ticked me off, and I packed up my stuff and drove away. As I passed George, I saluted him with my middle finger. I felt awful the moment I did it. George and Rene were the only two people who were going out of their way to help me. I kept driving then, but later I apologized to them over and over.

Everything in my life started going wrong again. I knew that if I didn't get it right, I'd end up dead or back in prison for life.

Pounding nails in a new roof helped me work out my mounting frustration. The way the pastor had gone after me felt too familiar and out of left field. It reminded me of the criticism and bullying from my family, which had to be the source of her anger, because I'd done nothing to provoke it.

I finished a row of shingles and stood, rolling my shoulders. Lifting my face to the warm afternoon sun, I accepted the fact that except for George and Rene's unfailing support, there was nothing left for me here. Without my kids and career, I felt at loose ends. What gave me the greatest joy was my music.

14

A NEW LIFE

I'd been out of jail for eight months when I called my parole officer. "I want to go to Nashville."

"When?"

"As soon as possible."

"Okay, you can go. I'll get you set up with a new parole officer, so check in when you get there."

I arrived in Nashville just as the sun set like a golden orb on the horizon over the city. While I'd hated leaving Rene, I felt relief with every mile that had separated me from the rest of my family. Their disgust and rejection put pressure on me that I didn't need.

In Nashville, I got a job working construction and connected with my parole officer.

It was a good thing I functioned well on four hours of sleep because I worked long hours to earn a living and spent most of each night working on my music. I also carved out time to learn the city and how the music industry worked.

Music Row was the heart of Nashville's entertainment business. Located southwest of downtown, it was home to numerous record labels, recording studios, publishing houses, video production companies, and licensing firms. I started a little music company there with an office and staff. I became a member of Broadcast Music Inc. and the American Society of Composers, Authors and Publishers.

I was shopping my music when George Strait's handlers contacted me.

They liked it.

"We really like your writing style," they explained, "but George doesn't like the bluesy stuff. Would you be willing to change it?"

I was too new to the industry to understand what they were offering. My answer should have been an enthusiastic, "Of course!"

Instead I said, "Let me think about it."

It took a while for me to understand that my blues influence wasn't going to work in Nashville. I separated my country music from my blues, shopping my blues in California and my country music in Nashville. I started a second recording studio outside of San Diego. I also had two music publishing companies, one for country and one for blues.

I picked up a client by the name of Johnny Fortune. Johnny had earned a gold record with RCA for his song "Little Red Dragster." I got rights to the record and republished it in Europe, making a ton of money. Johnny also recorded an album of my songs, which we released in Europe. I earned royalties from the songs I wrote and he sang. It was a sweet deal.

Still, as much as I enjoyed creating music, the longer I worked in Nashville, the less I liked the business side of things. Whenever I went to a big label with a client, the meetings started the same way.

With a long line of drugs on the conference table.

They'd snort cocaine while discussing business.

I disagreed with almost everything that Nashville stood for. They exploited people in the worst way, especially women. I tried working on the fringe of the industry without getting sucked into its mire. During those years, I was too exhausted to worry about who did or didn't love me. I only stayed in Nashville long enough to take care of business, and then I went to Austin until I had to go back. I liked Austin because it had a rich pool of talented people. I figured if I started over somewhere, it would be a good place to find exceptional employees.

"StevieRay," my friends warned, "you have to go to the right parties to work in this industry. You can't just leave town. And your hair's too short. To succeed, you need to fit in."

I'd already figured out there was a lot of money to be made in the music industry. I also knew that if I hung around that scene too long, it would suck me in.

After almost five years working in Nashville, I knew that if I stayed, the Lord would lift His hand off me. It was that simple. I closed my office, keeping all my songs, rights, royalties, and masters. Not sure what I would do next, I headed to Austin, Texas.

Austin was home to a music scene which centered, in part, around country and blues. Just because I was out of the music business didn't mean I didn't still enjoy it. The city was thriving, emerging as a center for business and technology. Twice when Luann and I had reinvented our lives, we'd chosen Texas to do it. Now it seemed as good a place as any for me to reinvent my life yet again. Besides, no cowboy was more at home than in Texas.

I started a talk radio program. I prerecorded interviews, played a lot of music, and did a couple of hours of talk radio each day. Long before Sean Hannity and Glen Beck were household names, I understood that it was important to pick controversial subjects to draw an audience. One of my favorite hot-button topics was homosexuality. Austin was liberal and had a large LGBTQ presence.

On air, I refused to refer to them as gay or homosexual. I infuriated my audience by referring to them as sodomites. While that may have been a correct biblical term, it garnered me an ongoing stream of death threats – and a lot of listeners. Austin was infuriated, and I had a large audience on the West Coast. My biggest audience, however, was Japan. The Japanese loved to listen to me argue.

A district attorney from California wrote to warn me that I might be violating the human rights of homosexuals. As far as I was concerned, sin was sin. I hated the homosexual lifestyle and was convinced that I was helping both society and God.

It took a while for God to show me the truth. All I'd done was discover a new way of tapping into the anger that I'd spent my life trying to contain. The Lord let me know that I was wrong and that I was judging my own sin as different than theirs. I realized that I was bullying them the same way my dad had bullied me.

That did it. I shut it down and got on my knees.

I figured I'd spent years doing things my way and making a big mess of my life. If I was going to follow Christ, I wouldn't do it halfway. I didn't want to be a man with one foot in the world and another in church. It was all or nothing for me. I wasn't going to try and see if the Bible was true. The outcome of my life would show that one way or another.

I wasn't so naïve as to think I'd get everything right, and I knew God didn't expect perfection. All I could do was give Him my heart, do my best, and trust Him with the rest. I'd accepted the fact that I wouldn't have a relationship with most of my family and some of my children unless God intervened.

My next order of business was to stop getting into toxic relationships with women. I'd fallen prey to that old pattern of behavior and married again in a hurry. I knew it was a mistake before the ink dried on the marriage license. I'd gotten out of the marriage and turned over a new leaf.

I lived alone, celibate, and didn't date.

I not only wanted to live a life pleasing to God, I wanted Him to teach me how to choose a woman for the right reasons.

Although I didn't date, sometimes on Wednesdays I went dancing. I was a good dancer and enjoyed it. I'd learned to enjoy those carefree evenings, but even then I was careful to stay away from women. I met a man who let me dance with his wife, Kathy, which was safe.

The dance floor was packed and rocked with boot-scootin' music when I arrived one evening. I saw Kathy walking toward me with a tall blonde in tow. My heart beat time with the music, and the lights backlit the blonde like a halo.

"StevieRay, this is Laura Sanchez," Kathy said with a grin like a Cheshire cat.

Time stood still for me as I looked into Laura's green eyes, the color I imagined a morning in Ireland might be. I had the uncanny feeling that she'd been sent to me by God. We danced, and then she left early to go home.

The next time we met at an ice cream parlor. I was going to make sure we took our time getting to know one another. I was already smitten by the time I realized that things would never work out for us. Laura held a master's degree in biology. She'd worked for fifteen years as a biologist and taught at a university.

When I met Laura, I was destitute. I lived in a garage apartment which had once been the maid's quarters behind someone's home. Laura was educated, a success in her field. Her parents weren't rich, but they had money in the bank.

I was flat broke.

Six months after we started dating, my truck was repossessed. I didn't know what she saw in me, but it wasn't the balance of my bank account.

"I don't care if I have ten dollars or ten million," she said. "As long as I have a kitchen and a bed, I'm happy."

She meant every word of it.

Laura was a well known biologist. She wrote books, taught, and spoke at symposiums. A true scientist, her office was stacked with specimens. She loved her work and enjoyed starting her day at five every morning and ending it at eight-thirty every evening. I felt sick at heart knowing that she would reconsider going out with me when she discovered the truth about me.

"Where did you graduate?" Laura asked one evening almost as an afterthought.

I let out a long sigh and spoke the bald truth. "Laura, I quit school after the eighth grade."

She looked at me and shrugged. "It doesn't matter," she said. "You're one of the smartest people I've ever known."

That ended the conversation. It didn't end the relationship, although I still had reservations. She knew nothing of my past or why my knees stayed sore from praying.

The first time I mentioned God, she made her position clear. "I'm a scientist," she said. "If something can't be proven, to me it doesn't exist."

I accepted her opinion without argument. I'd hated the way my father tried to browbeat me with the Bible. As far as I was concerned, God wasn't so much about an organization as about a relationship. God was about love. If she couldn't figure out I was different by my life, I needed to take a hard look at myself.

While I didn't talk to her about my beliefs, I did establish my boundaries. "I'll never just live with you," I explained. "It's not going to happen. I'm all about marriage and commitment."

I loved her brilliant mind and the way she poured herself into her work. She was kind and understanding. She never got angry or raised her voice. Our only disagreement was about getting married in a church.

"I came from a family of avid readers, especially my father,"

Laura explained. "We went to church until the day they had a book burning. They burned every book except the Bible. We never went back."

I never preached at her or tried to change her mind. It was more important to me that she see how I treated people. How I handled disappointments. How I handled money. I discovered that we were very much alike, and neither of us wanted or needed an extravagant lifestyle.

We married and moved into her modest older home. Built in the 1960s, it was a two-bedroom brick about a half-block walk from a lake. We were happy beyond our wildest dreams.

I have a fast metabolism and couldn't go from breakfast until lunch without food. I'd always needed to snack as many as ten times a day. That quirk in my dietary habits drove other women crazy. Laura understood. "You're hypoglycemic," she said. "I can deal with that." Without another word, she made sure I had healthy food to eat as often as I needed it. As a result, I felt better than I had in years. She took the time to get to know who I was and what I needed. Nobody in my life had ever done that.

One Sunday morning, Laura got up and said, "Let's go to church." We did and she never looked back. She embraced God, the Bible, and the church with the same open-arm affection that she used to embrace life. She remained a true scientist, but she put God first.

I knew that I needed to explain my past. We were walking along the lake one day as I thought about all the ugliness of my previous marriages and my family. I hated talking about it, but felt she had the right to know.

"I inherited a bad gene pool of pride," I said, trying to explain where I'd gone wrong.

"That's all in the past, so it's not relevant. Only the future matters."

For the first time in my life, I basked in unconditional love – from God and from my wife. I woke every day to a piece of heaven on earth. I knew that little by little, my past would be revealed, but I felt sure that Laura would recognize that I wasn't the same man as I'd been back then.

I wanted to start another oil company but felt uneasy about it, since Oscar Wyatt was alive and well – and right there in Texas.

After praying about it, I decided to start Austin Petroleum and stay as far as I could out of Oscar Wyatt's line of fire. This time I was determined to build the company right, keeping funds in reserve for times of economic downturns. I phoned a man I trusted. "I'm going to start an oil company," I explained. "And I need money."

His answer was short and sweet.

"How much?"

He sent me the money, and in 2002, I started Austin Petroleum Group. This time my goal was to build a successful company instead of a cash cow. Just about all I did was work on building the business. This time, I wanted every piece done right.

My reputation was a mixed bag. Some companies refused to do business with me. Others, like a pipeline group out of Tulsa, Oklahoma, rooted and cheered for me from day one.

It felt good to be back in the business. I set up shop and hired a CEO. Two years after starting the company, we were doing well. The first sign of trouble came when a group in Arkansas wrote us bad checks totaling $500,000.

In addition, we were pumping hundreds of gallons of gas to three truck stops owned by a group of Pakistanis. We made three drops a week, which meant that at the end of each week, they owed us a lot of money.

One weekend, they grabbed $500,000 in cash gas sales and skipped the country. As soon as I realized they'd left the US, I knew we wouldn't get that money back either. We were left owing a lot to our creditors. If that wasn't bad enough, when I shut down Austin Petroleum, my CEO drained the last $200,000 from our accounts and filed for bankruptcy.

I felt like I'd awoken to a nightmare. How could this be happening? This time, instead of taking matters into my own hands, I fell on my knees before God, begging Him to show me what to do. More than anything, I wanted to prove to everyone in the industry that I would do the right thing.

My biggest creditor was Valero, so my lawyer and I went to them in hopes of working out a payment plan. "Our money is 30 days past due, and we want it now. You went to prison once, and now you're trying to dupe us."

"No, I'm not," I insisted. "I'll pay you what I owe. Just let me set up payments."

They refused to do business with me and smeared my name in the industry. I wanted people to know that I wasn't a thief or a coward, so I went to talk to my creditors in Missouri, Arkansas, and Kansas. Each agreed to work out payment plans.

In time Valero agreed to accept payments of $10,000 a month. The payments almost strangled Laura and me, but we managed to come up with the money every month.

We never missed a single payment, which was noticed by the guys at Valero.

Five years into the payoff, I'd paid them just under $600,000, which was half of what we owed them. "He's been good," the top guy at Valero decided. "He's made his payments on time. As far as we're concerned, he's paid back what he owed. His partner owes the rest."

It felt like a huge weight had been lifted off my shoulders when they released me from any more payments. During the process, I'd regained trust in the industry. News – both good and bad – traveled fast.

I'd always heard that faith has no Plan B. I figured that must be right because I put together a new oil company, Southwest

Energy Group. I knew the business inside and out and made a million dollars off just one deal. That should have been a great start to a new business, but history had a way of repeating itself. This time it was my CPA who ripped us off. He paid his twenty-year-old son $1.4 million in consulting fees and drained the company dry.

My attorney was furious and wanted to sue. I prayed for weeks and months before deciding to walk away. I shut down the business and forgave the man. I figured that sometimes, it was best to let God and life deal with others.

15

THE PAST COMES CALLING

I stood in the pasture with my heifers one morning when my cell phone rang. I looked at the caller identification and answered with caution. The call was from my parents' phone. Since Dad had never called me, I assumed it was Mom. Somehow, I always held out the hope that she would say, "Son, you've made a lot of mistakes, but so have we. Let's put the past behind us. We love you."

"Hello?"

"This is your dad." Apprehension welled up in me, followed by a flash of anger. I forced myself to swallow it. Dad was a proud man, and calling me must have been one of the hardest things he'd ever done. I didn't want to take his dignity.

"Hello, Dad."

"We need money."

I was stunned. I knew by now that there wasn't enough money in the world to buy their affection. Their love wasn't available to me at any price. But finally, I had something they needed.

This was my chance to get back at them for the way they'd treated me.

All of a sudden, in my mind's eye, I pictured Joseph being sold into slavery. I followed his journey from Potiphar's house to prison. I remembered the way he'd become the most powerful man in Egypt aside from Pharaoh.

I imagined how Joseph must have felt watching his brothers standing in line for food during a famine. He could have exacted vengeance right then.

But he didn't.

Joseph forgave, realizing that what his brothers meant to destroy him, God had turned into a blessing that saved the entire family. There were two lessons I needed to learn from Joseph. One was simple: If Joseph could feed his family during a famine, I had to do the same for mine. But to do that, I needed to forgive my parents, especially my father. Not from my head, but like the Bible says, from my heart. I had no illusions that my generosity would clean the slate and earn me good will. But I had to forgive.

For years, I'd been asking them to forgive me. For the first time, I realized that hadn't been the right question. The question God wanted me to answer was this: *would I forgive them?*

That was a lot tougher than asking them to forgive me. It put the responsibility for forgiveness right back on my shoulders.

There in the pasture with cattle grazing beside me, for the first time in my life, I started the process of forgiving my father.

"I've kept a record over the years of how much it cost to raise you," he said. He began reciting numbers.

I listened, horrified. He'd kept an itemized list of what I cost him? It probably went all the way back to when I was a toddler and had to have that first surgery. *Lord, how many times is he going to hurt me this way?*

"That's enough," I said, stopping him. "Just get to the bottom line."

"Five thousand dollars."

I wanted to yell, "Let me tell you what I think of you! You'll never get a dime from me!" He'd been bullying me my whole life.

Still, I wouldn't allow myself to be disrespectful. I never belittled him about the money or wagged a finger.

A scripture drifted up from my mind. "Then Peter came to him and asked, 'Lord, how often should I forgive someone who sins against me? Seven times?'

"'No, not seven times,' Jesus replied, 'but seventy times seven.'"

I heaved a deep sigh. I'd known for years that I needed to forgive him, but I'd struggled with it. The way he'd treated me was *wrong*. There was no question about that. However, I understood that the Lord wanted me to forgive him now – and to just keep on forgiving as many times as it took.

"Okay."

The truth was that we didn't have money. We were living in an old one-bedroom, 700 square feet hunter's cabin. Finding an extra three hundred dollars would have been a stretch.

I found Laura. "We need to talk." We sent them two hundred to three hundred dollars a month, every month, and it was torturous. I was trying to rebuild my life and build the business, and we needed the money.

I didn't do it because I felt responsible. I did it because it was what Joseph did – and God required it.

The process of forgiveness began that day, but it was a journey. Every time they called and asked for more money, I suffered through days of tortured confusion and emotional pain. Just because I had forgiven them didn't mean I was happy with the situation.

Even though I never enjoyed talking to my dad, I figured out that forgiveness was a serious thing with God. In Matthew 18:35, the Bible tells about a man who didn't forgive, "...in his anger, his master turned him over to the jailers to be tortured, until he should repay all that he owed. That is how my heavenly Father will treat each of you, unless you forgive your brother from your heart."

I didn't know a lot about forgiveness, but I figured that

forgiving from the heart was a lot deeper work than forgiving from the head. It seemed to me that forgiving from the heart meant that I had to go as deep as the pain to get rid of that root. That's what I did.

Regardless of how I felt, I stuck with it, and in time I experienced a level of peace I'd never known in my life. For years I'd worked hard not to express anger, but it had been under the surface all along. Once I really forgave my parents, that simmering anger disappeared. For the first time in my life, I was at total peace. Another new emotion was the joy that bubbled out of me. If I'd understood the outcome, I would have forgiven years before.

I later learned that my parents were living on a total of twelve hundred a month from social security and had maxed out their credit cards. I'd had no idea that they were in such a financial mess.

I had forgiven Dad from my heart before he called for the last time. By now, we both knew that he was dying of cancer.

"I'm not going to apologize to you!" He shouted the words, loud and angry.

Stunned speechless, I couldn't think of anything to say.

"Did you hear me?" Dad demanded.

"Dad, I'm going to continue to pray for you."

That was our last conversation. The saddest part of my father's death was that it came as a relief to me. My biggest bully was finally gone. I would never have to take his bullying abuse again.

My dad was one of eleven children. There had been nine boys and two girls. They were so poor that there was never enough food for all of them. As a result, they had to fight to survive. Uncle

Ray, who'd helped me escape at fourteen, had been the youngest, and he left home at an early age.

Dad had learned to use anger to control people as a child. As an adult, he used anger to control everyone. I was like a whipped child to him my whole life. Right up to the day he took his last breath. It had been a huge revelation to me the day I'd realized that the anger controlling our relationship had been his. As far as I could tell, Dad hated every one of his brothers and sisters. That was his legacy. Not love, but bitterness and hatred.

Laura and I were asked to pay for Dad's funeral, which we did. Even though they worked to keep the costs low, it was a lot of money and a sacrifice to send.

"StevieRay," Rene asked, "would you and Laura please come to the funeral?"

"I'm not going to be a hypocrite, Rene. We never had a relationship, and I won't pretend we did. I've forgiven him, and that's all that matters to me."

Following Dad's death, my mother called. "Your dad said if I needed anything, to call you." We'd continued to send money, and by now we were sending six hundred dollars a month.

"I need more money," she demanded. When she called, it was always about money. If she didn't get her way, she went into bully mode. "I raised you for 14 years!" We continued sending her money, not always as much as she wanted, but we increased the amount until we sent her as much as five thousand dollars at times.

Rene called me, incensed. "Why do you send her that much money?" she asked. "All she does is call me and brag about it."

"She said she needs it."

"She's carrying a *Gucci bag* on her walker! She bought it with the money you sent!"

Aunt Gail, my mother's sister, questioned my mother about it. "Why do you lean on StevieRay so heavy for financial help?"

"All the trouble that boy caused us over the years?" Mom asked. "He can never repay me."

"I'm starting a new oil company in Houston," I told Laura in 2007. She asked the question I'd come to expect.

"How many times are you going to do this?"

"Until God helps me find the right person."

That same year, I started Gulf Coast Energy, LLC.

Laura and I were both shocked at how people we'd trusted had become so dishonest when large sums of money were on the line. I'd become wary, distrusting. I wasn't sure that anyone without the Lord Jesus at the center of their life could be trusted with access to millions of dollars. Until I found someone that could, I would run the company on my own.

We were living on seventy acres near Mason, Texas, at the time, and I had a corporate condo in Houston. I didn't have any desire to live in the city, and neither did Laura. Every Sunday after church, I drove to Houston to work, spending nights at the condo. The long hours, hard work, and time spent away from home took a toll, but I didn't know anyone I trusted enough to hand the reins of the company.

"Honey, we have to move to Houston," Laura insisted. I knew she was right. If she was there, I'd eat better, spend less time on the road, and get more rest. I explained how suffocating I found Houston. How much I looked forward to driving home Thursday evening. How I drank in the country air like an elixir. How the quiet sounds of our cattle soothed my soul. Having Laura there in our modest home on seventy acres revived me, giving me the strength to go back for another week...and another.

Dealing in commodities required a different kind of thinking than was needed in many businesses. Strange as it seemed with my learning disabilities, my mind operated that way. I knew I had the skills to build a monster business. Even so, I didn't so much as incorporate until the Lord prompted me that it was time. Instead of trusting my own judgment, I bathed every decision in prayer. I also made a conscious choice to deal with problems and conflict by the power of the Spirit rather than the arm of the flesh.

I didn't want to make any of the same mistakes I'd made before. That meant several things. It meant that I refused to micromanage my employees. The way I saw it, the need to micromanage stemmed from fear and the need to control. I'd been there and done that, and it wasn't a strategy for success.

I refused to make any decision without waiting on direction from God – no matter how intense the pressure.

I refused to let anything move me out of peace. Jesus paid a high price for peace, and I determined to live every day in it. Which meant I had to let go of upsets and anger. There were already enough bullies in the world. From terrorists to Shot Callers on a prison yard to neighborhood bullies, they came in all shapes and sizes. My dad had been a bully. He hadn't used his fists; he'd used his words to bully.

I'd bullied my employees and business associates before I went to prison, and I refused to do it again. Whenever I had a choice, I moved in the opposite direction from my father's behavior.

Doing things God's way, within a few years I'd turned my struggling company into a success.

16

A NEW ENDING

My cell phone vibrated against the boardroom table for the tenth time in an hour. I apologized and excused myself from the room. I was out of state at a business meeting while one of my employees was back home handling a twenty million-dollar deal. He was scared out of his mind that he would mess up.

The last thing I wanted was to find myself upside down on a deal that large. However, I'd prayed it through and had clear direction from the Lord. He gave me the green light for the project but specified that this employee was the one to handle it.

"You can do this," I assured him. "Just remember that I'm praying for you."

The deal went well and when it was over, the employee had more confidence.

My employees called me The Shepherd because I spent so much time in prayer.

I liked this new title. It felt good to guide, like a shepherd.

Owning any business, especially an oil company, meant being bombarded with opportunities to get into fear. I refused to do it. I knew that fear was a tool of the devil, and any decision I made prompted by fear would be wrong. My goal was to operate in complete faith. Once I was convinced that God wanted me to do something, I was fearless.

My Chief Financial Officer appeared puffed up and pompous as he marched into my office one day and put a spreadsheet on my desk. "We're going broke!" he announced.

I didn't take the bait. "We have money in the bank," I said in a voice so soft it was almost a whisper.

"Sure, we do now. But if you'll look at these projections, you'll see that in six months, we'll be in trouble. Out of respect to your employees, you should call everyone together and tell them you're going broke."

"I don't think so."

"What do you intend to do?"

"Wait on God and watch Him do a miracle."

My CFO gathered up his spreadsheets and huffed out of my office. I refused to get into fear, and neither would I micromanage him. I took the situation to God in prayer.

Six months later, we had a balanced budget. We weren't even close to going broke.

I let my CFO go.

On another occasion, I'd been in negotiations with Shell Oil and American Airlines in a one hundred-million dollar deal to buy jet fuel. It looked sweet, but when I crunched the numbers, it didn't work. In addition, I didn't have a green light from God. So I bowed out of the deal.

People got crazy when millions of dollars were on the line. Afterwards, the trader called, irate.

"I'm killing you!" he screamed. The sound of gunfire blasted through the telephone. I wasn't afraid. In fact, I found him entertaining.

"I know where you live!" he shouted. "I'm coming for you!"

"Let me make sure you have the right address." I reeled it off without an ounce of fear.

When I got off the phone, I prayed for the guy. He needed help.

I'd figured out that until I learned to control distractions, I would never be able to do what God called me to do.

Once the company had grown to a good size, I wanted to buy land and cattle. Laura and I searched for a long time before we found our little piece of paradise. I wanted flat land to graze cattle. Laura wanted a house with a view, and the two didn't seem to mix.

"I wonder if we can find a compromise," Laura said one day. "What if we found a house and property to live on and bought the rest of the acreage we need close by? I've arranged for our realtor to take us to look at a house on 200 acres, just to give us a point of reference."

I walked up to the two-story house on a hill and dropped into a seat on the covered porch. The view was breathtaking. "I'll take it," I announced.

"I don't want a two-story house," Laura said, stunned.

"I want to buy this place," I said. "While it's only 200 acres, we can buy other property nearby to ranch."

"Could we at least look inside?" Laura asked.

I had known I was home the moment I sat on the porch and looked out over the hills. Horses in the corral and cattle in the pastures gave me an overwhelming sense of peace. Like me, Laura loved the land. As a biologist, she found that central Texas was like a huge lab with thousands of plant specimens. Nothing made her happier than finding plants that had never been recorded in the area and registering them.

From the time we moved to the property, Laura worked from daylight to dark. In addition to helping me run the ranch, she took care of her gardens and cooked all our food. We raised our own grass-fed beef, and Laura made her own bread.

For Christmas, Laura asked for a cow, so she'd have fresh milk.

"An animal that size could hurt you," I said. "How about a goat?"

I bought her goats, which she milked twice a day.

Whenever I left town, Laura filled an ice chest with home-grown food. She didn't want me to eat processed food on the road. She banned sugar from our diet, and I didn't miss it. She made decadent ice cream with real cream.

Over the years, I had reconnected with Jason, Justin, and Cody, my sons with Doris. Doris never kicked her drug habit. Thirteen years after our divorce, she was found dead with a knife in her chest. Because she'd been in and out of rehab, the medical examiner ruled her death a suicide – although she was living in a volatile relationship with a drug dealer at the time.

The boys lived through a childhood that made mine look like a walk in the park. Jason, like his mother, struggled with drug addictions. Four years after his mother's death, he committed suicide.

I couldn't wrap my head around the kind of inner turmoil that would trigger suicide. I mourned my son – and my grandson who would never know his father. It seemed as though Doris' demons had chased him into an early grave.

I never heard from Luann again. My two sets of twins are in their late 20s now, and the tragedy of my life is that I don't know them. I pray that God will restore them to me one day.

My old nemesis, Oscar Wyatt, Jr. – the man who made sure I went to prison – made international news when he was indicted on five criminal counts. Following Saddam Hussein's invasion of

Kuwait in 1990, the United Nations imposed sanctions on Iraq. In short, it was illegal to buy oil from Iraq.

In 1996, they agreed on a compromise. Iraqi oil profits would be put in a UN escrow account to be used for humanitarian purposes. Saddam was allowed to handpick his customers. Of course, his old friend Oscar Wyatt was among the chosen.

However, four years later, Saddam decided he wasn't making enough profit. To compensate, he demanded bribes – which he called surcharges – from his customers. According to prosecutors, Oscar Wyatt set up companies overseas which paid bribes. He continued doing business with Iraq illegally.

Following a grueling trial in New York, Oscar pled guilty to the charges. At age 83, the man who got me sent to prison was in prison himself.

As I followed Oscar's trial and sentencing in the news, I realized that except for the grace of God, I would have ended up just like him. Still chasing the almighty dollar at any cost into my old age.

Oscar had a pretty rough start when his alcoholic father abandoned the family, leaving him to be raised by a single mother. He flew combat missions during World War II. Later he started Coastal Corporation and became a billionaire.

Oscar Wyatt had more money than he could have spent in multiple lifetimes. He didn't need money. I suspected that greed had gotten a stranglehold on him, and he was addicted to the power money could buy.

Although I'd never accumulated the kind of wealth Oscar did, I knew too well what the love of money could do to a man. I never believed that money was bad in and of itself. Money was just a tool. The big question was not if a person had money. It was if the money had the person. At one time, money had Oscar and me both.

I was grateful that God had changed me.

I didn't know about Oscar, but my life had been marked by

the anger that had simmered beneath the surface all the time, especially in my twenties and thirties. The anger erupted in a lot of fights. I'd even beaten up Wayne. I knew there was something wrong with me, but I had no idea what it was. In an effort to find out, I'd read every self-help book on the market. During my rodeo years, I didn't always have money to buy books, so we'd stop at a bookstore in one town, and I'd read until it was time to leave. The next time we stopped, I'd find the same book and pick up where I'd left off. I didn't find my answers in self-help books. I had religion but without faith, it was a terrible thing.

Everything changed when I developed a relationship with Jesus. I put my trust in God and believed the Bible, reading it daily. I worked from biblical principles. I tithed and gave and made a lot of money, but something always went wrong.

I realized that there was a powerful connection between forgiveness and prosperity. When I finally forgave my parents from my heart, it seemed as though whatever had blocked great prosperity in my life became unplugged.

I still tithed. I gave offerings. I invested money back into the business. I put money into savings. I gave huge amounts of money to widows and orphans, and I made a startling discovery.

I couldn't give it all away.

God kept multiplying it back to me.

Forgiveness changed everything.

I had business associates who graduated from Harvard and Yale who couldn't understand how my life had turned out so well. That was an interesting question. I remembered being beat up every day by gangs of bullies – certain that I'd die at their hands.

I remembered dropping out of school after eighth grade and driving across country alone. I thought back to all those wonderful years riding the rodeo circuit and finding friends who were more faithful than family.

I thought back to Luann and the mob. To training horses for

Robert and learning the oil business. To living life on the run from authorities and from the Mafia.

I recalled the rabid quest for money and the sickening realization that there would never, ever be enough. I thought about those years in a maximum-security prison. The certainty that nothing good could come out of the mess I'd made of my life.

"There's only one answer," I told my associates from Yale and Harvard.

They looked at me with blank stares.

"Jesus," I said. "He's the reason my life turned out this way."

This is what I knew: While I was in the pit of despair, I cried out to God. When that happened, Jesus rewrote a whole new ending to my life.

17

GIVING BACK

"I want to start an orphanage," I told Laura over dinner one evening. "Not necessarily an orphanage, but something like that."

"That's real hard, Honey," Laura replied. "Let's just donate to one."

That didn't seem like enough to me. I couldn't help but wonder what would have happened to me without Buck and the other cowboys who became like family. Without men like Robert who kept stepping into my life to help me.

I'd been a tither and a giver for years, supporting organizations like Feed the Children. Laura and I had given to many good causes such as Christians United for Israel, Samaritan's Purse, our local fire department, relief organizations, and political candidates. But when I read the Bible, I learned the importance of giving to widows and orphans. In time, we focused on giving to orphanages and various charities that helped kids that had fallen through society's cracks. Both of us wanted to give to programs closer to home, but there weren't many.

I wasn't an orphan, of course. But I didn't have parents who loved me or were interested in supporting me. For all practical purposes, I considered myself an orphan. The term I used to describe myself more often was a throwaway kid. It seemed to me that in our society, more and more children were being tossed out like yesterday's trash.

The largest group of throwaway kids in our country seemed to be those in the foster care system. The system was designed to provide short term protection against abuse and neglect —a worthy goal. What it didn't do was provide a long-term solution. It didn't equip children with the skills they would need to survive once they'd aged out of the system, usually at age 18.

The more I learned about the plight of the kids leaving foster care, the more concerned I became. Most of them didn't have a support system. One study found that within a year of leaving the foster care system, sixty-six percent of them were homeless, in jail, or dead. A staggering eighty percent of the prison population had come out of foster care. Girls in foster care were six hundred percent more likely than their peers to get pregnant before age twenty-one.

Nineteen percent of boys leaving foster care and fifteen percent of girls would be sentenced to prison within two years of leaving the system. That didn't mean they were bad kids. It just meant that they had no support system, no education, and no skills to support themselves.

Two to five years after leaving foster care, young men were imprisoned at a rate of twenty-two percent and women at twenty percent. After more than five years out of the foster care system, fifty-five percent of the males and a staggering sixty-three percent of the females were incarcerated.

In a study of housing arrangements for kids leaving foster care, twenty-five percent of boys and twenty-nine percent of girls had nowhere to go. They were homeless. A year later, the numbers jumped to thirty-five percent of the boys and forty-three percent of the girls who were homeless.

Their plight broke my heart. As far as I was concerned, the

most immediate need Laura and I could fill was to help provide a home, a support system, education, or training in a skill for those kids aging out of foster care.

I started spending two to three hours in prayer every morning and afternoon asking God for direction. The number of kids living on the streets and ending up in prison was a blight on our society. I wanted to figure out a way to give them not a handout but a hand up.

One of my friends adopted a thirteen-year-old boy whose parents had given him away. Bart gave the boy a home, stability and love, but the boy didn't respond well.

"I love that kid," Bart told me. "I've given him a good home for five years. I feed him and clothe him. I put my arms around him and tell him that he's loved. Why isn't that enough?"

"Because he's in horrible emotional pain," I said. "He's heart-broken and enraged that his parents gave him away. Your love and the home you've given him don't negate that. It doesn't fix it."

Bart released a long sigh. "I admit that I don't understand, but I know you do. Will you talk to him?"

I got it that Bart didn't understand. If someone hadn't experienced rejection by the people who'd brought them into the world, it would be hard to imagine the pain and rage it brought.

I met with the boy and told him about my life. I told him that the pain and anger had almost derailed me numerous times. Once he knew that I'd felt that pain and tasted that anger, I told him what I wished someone had told me.

"You'll probably never know why your parents didn't keep you," I said. "But what you've got to understand is that what they did is their problem. It's on them. It's not on you. None of this was your fault. You didn't cause it, and you can't fix it. But the emotional pain, the anger and the rage, will never stop until you forgive them. Forgiving them doesn't mean that what they did was right. It just means you're not going to let the bitterness derail your life."

We talked for a long time, and he understood. It seemed to help a lot, but working through these emotional landmines and forgiving is a process that doesn't happen overnight. During the day, he could focus on all the good things in his life. Alone at night, memories reached up from the past like a specter sent to destroy his joy. The best he could do was try and control the anger that festering pain had caused. Until he forgave them, he was powerless to stop the torment he felt.

These kids need more than a bed to sleep in and food on the table. Love isn't even enough. They need to make sense of the pain that simmers into rage over their circumstances. More than anything, they need a mentor who will lead them to Jesus. Someone to help them begin the process of forgiving—because that's the first step to becoming whole.

Randy, our realtor, stayed on the lookout for land within driving distance of our ranch. In late fall of 2016, he called to tell me about a property he'd seen.

"I found 600 acres adjacent to the Rocky Creek acreage," Randy said. "Not sure if it'll work for you because it has all these buildings on it."

"What were the buildings for?"

"It was a church retreat."

"I'd like to see it."

Randy and I drove under a metal archway which read in large letters, *LAZY H*.

"Years back, a man named Harris was traveling through the Hill Country and saw this land," Randy explained. "He felt called to build a church retreat, so that's what he did. Set it up for either weekly or weekend stays. He ran it for years, but the family has decided to sell it. As you know, deer hunting is very profitable. They've been offered many times over their asking price to turn it into a place for hunting deer. The family won't sell it to them. That's not what they want it used for."

Randy showed me a foreman's house, a huge pavilion with a stage, an auditorium, a recreational area, a swimming pool, and cabins, each with bedrooms, bathrooms, and a kitchen. The wooded property sloped down to a rushing creek. High on the bluff above us stood a little cabin with a loft prayer room. There was also a cross which could be lit at night.

We drove up the bluff and I looked down on one of the most beautiful pieces of land I'd ever seen. The buildings needed repairs, but what I saw there was a transitional home for young men leaving the foster care system or an orphanage. I could see it filled with young men 18 and up who were at a crossroads in their lives. It would take a lot of money, but I knew if this was God's plan, He'd make a way.

"We could teach them life skills," I told Laura.

"Like how to have a healthy relationship," she said.

"How to balance a checkbook and manage their money," I added. "We wouldn't force an agenda on them. We'd let them figure out what they wanted to do with their lives, and we'd help them reach their goals."

If a young man wanted to become a carpenter, a doctor, a lawyer, or a janitor, it wouldn't matter. We'd help him get there. If someone wanted to be a rodeo cowboy, I'd mentor him. If they needed a trade school, we'd get them in one. If they needed college, we'd find a way.

Some of them might just need ninety days to de-stress. Others might be there for a long time, depending on their goals. It would vary from person to person.

More than anything, I wanted to teach them how to handle the pain – and how to forgive. I wanted to see them having fun while learning to structure their lives in the direction they wanted to go.

When God gave me a green light to buy the Lazy H, I was ready for a change. I sold Gulf Coast Energy and used a portion of the proceeds to buy the property. News of what I was going to do with the place spread through town like a grassfire, and folks were happy about it. Everywhere I went, people had stories to tell about how their lives had been impacted at the Lazy H.

"I was baptized there!" I heard over and over.

I explained that I wanted to bring in kids not just from Texas but from places as far away as New York and New Jersey. I wanted the staff to be led by the Lord but without any finger wagging. That never helped anyone. I hoped to house 150 young people on the property without taking any state or federal funds. If it was done right, I figured a lot of people would help keep it going. My dream was to expand in time to several more facilities.

18

YOUR JOURNEY

A brisk wind pushed me down the slope as I walked around the Lazy H and inspected the changes that would transform a church camp into a home for young adults. It felt good to be doing something to help kids without a family support system. I sat on a boulder overlooking a creek and pondered the journey that had brought me here.

Looking back, I realized that pain and anger created the engine that drove my life off the tracks. Although that was my experience, the truth was that nobody makes it through life unscathed. There's a lot of evil in the world, and it comes in many shapes and sizes.

Children and adults have been beaten, burned with cigarettes, sexually molested, and gang raped. Kids have been sold into sexual slavery, prostituted on the streets and in brothels. Horrific things happen every day. You may have lived through such things. Whatever your story, there are things in life that hurt.

No matter who you are, where you've been, or what you've been through—there is hope for you.

Somebody loved you so much that He died for you. That person is Jesus. He wants to make you whole, happy, and successful.

One of the most amazing things about Jesus is that He paid the price for your sins and mine, before we were born. Do you know what that means?

You're forgiven.

God forgave you, and your path to freedom from pain is to forgive. Let me repeat: Forgiving those who hurt you doesn't make what they did right. They might need to be held accountable to the law, and that's okay. Behavior has consequences. They will also be held accountable to God.

A lot of people refuse to forgive because they don't want to give up their right to be angry. You have the right to be angry. Just realize that holding onto the anger also holds the pain in place. It keeps you frozen in the same cycle of misery and hurt.

The other thing refusing to forgive does is hold you in a victim mentality. I never could stand being a victim. Still can't. Don't give anyone that kind of power over your life. When you forgive, you take back the power of your past to hurt you. You take back control over your emotions.

Forgiveness will take you from being a victim to being a victor.

I'm not saying you can't achieve success without forgiving. I did, and you can too. But unforgiveness makes success so much harder. Why? Because you're dragging around a ball and chain of emotional anger and pain, which affects you every day.

I know this by experience.

I also want to clarify that while forgiving those who hurt you won't change your past, it *will* change your future.

If I'd known years ago that the secret to living free of pain and in peace was forgiving, my life would have been different. It took me a long time to get here. My hope is that it won't take you that long.

It's hard for me to describe the difference that forgiving can bring. It's like winning a lottery ticket. You can hold onto that ticket—with all it promises—or you can cash it in and claim your new life.

ABOUT THE AUTHOR

StevieRay Hansen, owner and founder of Gulf Coast Energy LLC, is more than just a corporate businessman. Learning disabled and suffering from ADHD, he was rejected by his family and traveled across the country alone at age 14. Without the love and direction of a father, Hansen suffered through the school of hard knocks. His bigger-than-Texas entrepreneurial spirt expressed itself as a rodeo champ, rancher, cattleman and songwriter.

Hansen became a multimillionaire, and then lost it all as the price of oil plummeted. When the bottom fell out of the oil industry, StevieRay was prosecuted and went to prison for the white-collar crime of floating bad checks. It was there that he met Jesus and was transformed into a new creature in Christ. According to Psalm 68:5-6, God revealed Himself to StevieRay as the Father to the fatherless—the One who sets the lonely in families and leads prisoners out of captivity and into prosperity.

With a Father to lead and guide him through the mountains and valleys of life, Hansen met and married his wife, Laura, a biologist for the Department of Defense. He started Gulf Coast Energy, and God taught him how to be a spiritual leader in his home and business. His heart's desire is to help displaced children who feel lost and alone, giving them a helping hand.

For more information...

www.the127.org
stevieray@the127.org

StevieRay Hansen
1406 E Main Street, Suite 267
Fredericksburg, TX 78624

94304679R00079

Made in the USA
Lexington, KY
26 July 2018